CHARLES MACIEJEWSKI was born in East Lothian 65 years ago and has spent most of his life in Scotland on both the east and west coasts. He currently lives on the outskirts of Inverness. He served in the British Army and the Scottish Police Service prior to working in the Middle East for a number of years. He enjoys spending his retirement touring Scotland with his wife and researching the places he visits through old books and journals, an activity which provided the inspiration for this book.

# SCOTLAND
# THE WORST

*A Derogatory Guide to the Worst Places to Visit in Times Gone By*

Introduced and compiled by
CHARLES MACIEJEWSKI

**Luath** Press Limited
EDINBURGH
www.luath.co.uk

First published 2019

ISBN: 978-1-912147-92-2

The author's right to be identified as author of this book under the
Copyright, Designs and Patents Act 1988 has been asserted.

The paper used in this book is recyclable. It is made from low chlorine pulps
produced in a low energy, low emission manner from renewable forests.

Typeset in 12 point P22MayflowerSmooth by Lapiz

Printed and bound by Martins the Printers Ltd., Berwick-upon-Tweed

# CONTENTS

# INTRODUCTION

Tour guides to Scotland usually start with a summary of the many delights that our country has to offer and there are many, not least the wonderful scenery and occasional periods of fine weather that allow one to actually see it. Here's what an early writer had to say about our bonnie wee country and her inhabitants:

> If the air was not pure and well refined by its agitation, it would be so infected with the stinks of their towns, and the steams of the nasty inhabitants, that it would be pestilent and destructive... The thistle was wisely placed there, partly to show the fertility of the country, nature alone producing plenty of these gay flowers, and partly as an emblem of the people, the top thereof having some colour of a flower, but the bulk and substance of it, is only sharp, and poisonous pricks.

KIRKE, T, *A modern account of Scotland being an exact description of the country, and a true character of the people and their manners*, 1679.

The works of Robert Burns and Sir Walter Scott did much to romanticise Scotland. Roads improved, the railways arrived and the visits by Queen Victoria and Prince Albert (and their purchase of Balmoral Castle in 1852) confirmed Scotland as a worthwhile tourist destination. There are now numerous guides available and, as a holiday destination, it rivals anywhere in the world – so much so that it often features in 'best places to visit' guides and articles.

Whilst it is always nice to read complimentary things about our country and ourselves, this, being an alternative guide, will concentrate on the less generous comments and views, scurrilous though they may seem.

The best known and oft-quoted travellers were Johnson and Boswell, who toured our fair land in 1773, but there were others before and since. This guide is a compendium of critical comments made by visitors to Caledonia from the 17th to the 19th centuries. Tourists during this period were generally wealthy and well-educated and some wrote books about their tours which often reflected their social, political and religious views, as well as their opinions about what they observed during their travels. Some were most likely deliberately insulting or satirical and reflective of the political tensions that existed between Scotland and England at the time. The authors quoted hailed not just from England and Scotland but also from Wales, Northern Ireland, America, Switzerland and Germany.

Scotland is renowned for whisky, golf and fine food – not forgetting its two most enduring symbols, kilts and bagpipes. Our travellers expressed opinions about all these things, as well as the people and the quality of the accommodation. Whilst today we are spoiled for choice in respect of the information available to budding visitors, the paucity of guide books then meant that great reliance was placed on those few that were available, which created a vision of Scotland and the Scots that, rightly or wrongly, determined the manner in which the country and people were viewed. I have selected what I consider to be the best of the worst.

It is hoped that modern-day visitors will find the places depicted much changed - and mostly for the better! Those of Scottish descent may feel inclined to arm themselves with a claymore and dirk but, instead, let us join together and have a smile, a chuckle and an outright laugh as to the manner in which Scotland and its people were once viewed. After all, as Scotland's national bard, Robert Burns, once observed:

> O wad some Power the giftie gie us
> To see oursels as ithers see us!

# NOTES ON LANGUAGE

The quotes are all replicated as they were written, except that current spellings of words and places have been updated to their current form.

The Gazetteer entries are listed under the old counties of Scotland, as opposed to the current council areas, the former being the means by which the quoted correspondents identified their locations.

The reader will see references to 'Sawney', which, in a Scottish etymological dictionary of 1825, stated that 'Sandie' was an abbreviation of Alexander – 'Hence the English seemed to have formed their ludicrous national designation of Sawney for a Scotsman.' An English etymological dictionary of 1846 defines Sawney as 'a silly, stupid fellow – a sarcastic designation for a native of Scotland.' The description is no longer in use.

# GAZETTEER

# Aberarder, Loch Laggan, Inverness-shire

The inn itself bore a close resemblance to a post house... It had originally been intended for a hunting box; but no care having been taken to keep it in repair, it was now fast hastening to decay. The walls of the rooms were dripping with damp and mildew; the flooring of the best room was broken up; and the night wind sighed mournfully through the innumerable fractures in the roof. It was, on the whole, in point of accommodation, a very miserable place.

SUTHERLAND, A, *A Summer Ramble in the North Highlands*, Edinburgh, 1825.

# Aberdeen City, Aberdeenshire

Their manufacture is chiefly in stockings... and every morning the poor bring in loads to sell about the town... They are generally all white, when they bring them in, and exceedingly cheap; and the maid servants scour them by treading them in lye, in a large tub, which gives the strangers great diversion, for by so doing they are obliged to expose their legs and thighs, by holding up their coats sometimes rather too high.

VOLUNTEER, *A Journey through part of England and Scotland... in the year 1746*, London, 1747.

I went out after breakfast very willing to admire said Union Street, but could not get my admiration up to the required mark. True, the houses form two very long lines, but the buildings are low, and the dull grey granite is by no means pleasant to look upon.

WELD, C, *Two months in the Highlands, Orcadia, and Skye*, London, 1860.

Note book further makes particular attention of the fish-wives, a race of mighty ruddy-cheeked women, any one of whom would be a match in tongue, probably as well as muscle, for three ordinary city bred men.

WELD, C, *Two months in the Highlands, Orcadia, and Skye*, London, 1860.

A statue has also been erected in Castle Street... in honour of the late Duke of Gordon; a base and despicable, but, from manner, rather a popular fellow. A bad statue, but still very ornamental of a street... We had a beastly Circuit dinner, on a sanded floor, and came eagerly away this morning from the stinking Royal Hotel.

COCKBURN, H, *Circuit Journeys by the late Lord Cockburn*, Edinburgh, 1889.

# Aberdeenshire

Before leaving Banffshire, however, we cannot refrain from paying a tribute to the prosperous appearance and civil deportment of its peasantry. In apparel, in cleanliness, and even in expression of countenance, they are infinitely superior to the boors of Aberdeenshire.

SUTHERLAND, A, *A Summer Ramble in the North Highlands*, Edinburgh, 1825.

## Aberfeldy, Perthshire

Aberfeldy is a place that might properly be called Aberfilthy, for marvellously foul it is. You enter through a beggarly street and arrive at a dirty inn.

SOUTHEY, R, *Journal of a tour in Scotland in* 1819, London, 1929.

## Aberfoyle, Perthshire

The Clachan itself is but a miserable fifth rate inn... the very look of which made us abandon our first intention of passing the night there... At length, the not very gracious landlady condescended to bring us some cold lamb, which tasted almost as musty as the room smelt, and some vinegar not quite as sour as her own looks.

TOWNSHEND, C, *A Descriptive Tour of Scotland*, London, 1840.

## Aboyne, Aberdeenshire

Still exhibits all the signs of dilapidation and insolvency. But while his woods are failing, and railways are waiting to sleep upon them, the contemptible old monkey faced wretch of a beau, who danced at Versailles with Marie Antoinette about sixty years ago, is still grinning and dancing somewhere abroad, at the expense of creditors who can't afford to let him die.

COCKBURN, H, *Circuit Journeys by the late Lord Cockburn*, Edinburgh, 1889.

# Achanalt, by Garve, Ross and Cromarty

We went into the inn at Achanalt, a miserable place, bad as a Gallician posada, or an estallagem in Algarve... The house, wretched as it was, was not without some symptoms of improvement; there was the crank of a bell in the dirty, smoked, un-plastered wall, showing that it was intended to fit up the room.

SOUTHEY, R, *Journal of a tour in Scotland in 1819*, London, 1929.

# Achnasheen, Ross and Cromarty

The inn, moreover, as it is called, is the most deplorable I have ever been within, worse by far than either Letterfinlay or Shiel House. No party of ladies could put up here... While our hideous dinner was preparing, I walked to the top of a hill.

COCKBURN, H, *Circuit Journeys by the late Lord Cockburn*, Edinburgh, 1889.

# Altnaharra, Sutherland

## Inn

This inn is miserable in the extreme.

ANDERSON, G & ANDERSON, P, *Guide to the Highlands and Islands of Scotland*, London, 1834.

# Angus

We did not find so kind a reception among the common people of Angus, and the other shires on this side the country, as the Scots usually give to strangers: but we found it was because we were Englishmen.

DEFOE, D, *A tour thro' the whole Island of Great Britain*, London, 1727.

# Annan, Dumfriesshire

The face of trade is altered since that time, and by the ruins of the place the merchants, and men of substance, removed to Dumfries, the town continues, to all appearance, in a state of irrevocable decay.

DEFOE, D, *A tour thro' the whole Island of Great Britain*, London, 1727.

# Appin, Argyllshire

Appin is a miserable looking place.

CARR, J, *Caledonian Sketches or A Tour through Scotland in 1807*, London, 1809.

# Arbroath, Angus

Arbroath, as a town, is entirely destitute of attraction. It is huddled together without plan, and built of a dull reddish sandstone, extremely irritating to the eye. A fetid rivulet, fringed with spinning mills, flows through it.

SUTHERLAND, A, *A Summer Ramble in the North Highlands*, Edinburgh, 1825.

Is not good.

COCKBURN, H, *Circuit Journeys by the late Lord Cockburn*, Edinburgh, 1889.

And here at Arbroath I saw more prostitutes walking the streets than would I think have been seen in any English town of no greater extent or population.

SOUTHEY, R, *Journal of a tour in Scotland in 1819*, London, 1929.

# Ardersier, Inverness-shire

A place consists of numbers of very mean houses, owing its life and support to the neighbouring fort.

PENNANT, T, *A Tour in Scotland 1769*, London, 1771.

A paltry village.

BOTFIELD, B, *Journal of a Tour Through the Highlands of Scotland during the Summer of 1829*, Edinburgh, 1830.

# Ardgour, Argyllshire

The present writer has seen a stout old fellow, of the very lowest class, in Ardgour, take his wife and daughter, with wicker baskets on their backs, to a dunghill, fill their baskets with manure, and send them to spread it with their hands on the croft; then, with his great coat on, lay himself down on the lee side of the heap, to bask and chew tobacco till they returned for another load.

BURT, E & JAMIESON, R, *Letters from a Gentleman in the North of Scotland to his friend in London*, London, 1818.

# Arisaig, Inverness-shire

I was soon surrounded by the various naval characters, who expected to extract as many guineas out of the Sassenach as he should prove silly enough to give. One of these Vikings, half drunk, his mouth streaming tobacco from each angle, desired to know if I was the gentleman who wished to carry a horse to Skye.

MacCULLOCH, J *The Highlands and Western Isles of Scotland*, London, 1824.

A poor looking village, scattered along the shores of a bay.

TOWNSHEND, C, *A Descriptive Tour of Scotland*, London, 1840.

## Arisaig Inn

Being conducted to an apartment upstairs, we found there a blackguard looking fellow eating herring and drinking whisky, the mingled fumes whereof were so intolerable that we made a rush into the open air, and, on finding that we could have no other sitting room, our disposition to remain was considerably abated.

TOWNSHEND, C, *A Descriptive Tour of Scotland*, London, 1840.

We arrived at Arisaig, which is so unusual a route anywhere, that the inn keeper seemed in as much consternation at the arrival of travellers, as if we had been comets, or had rode upon broomsticks... Here being allowed by special licence to partake of some refreshment, we 'tea'd,' though certainly the tea was not from Assam or from the Emperor of China's own tea chest, but came, more probably, off the neighbouring hedges or hay-fields.

SINCLAIR, C, *Scotland and the Scotch*, New York, 1840.

# Aros, Isle of Mull, Argyllshire

After ringing and ordering supper at least twenty times, we gave up the matter in pure despair, and at last actually went supperless to bed. The next morning, the girl apologised for our having been so badly waited on, and accounted for it by telling us that all the time we had been ringing and scolding, her mistress was bringing forth a man child into the world.

TOWNSHEND, C, *A Descriptive Tour of Scotland*, London, 1840.

# Arrochar, Dunbartonshire

On our arrival at the front door, a servant came out and without saying with 'your leave sir,' directed the driver to go round to the other side of the house, where we were shown into a smoky, dirty room... we turned short upon our heels and directed the baggage to be again put into the cart, leaving the servant to stammer out an apology... I hope that none of my countrymen at least, will ever pay a sous to the landlord at Arrochar.

CARTER, N, *Letters from Europe comprising The Journal of a Tour through... Scotland... in 1825*, New York, 1827.


# Auchterarder, Perthshire

We breakfasted at an incommodious and dirty inn.

HERON, R, *Observations made in a journey through the Western Counties of Scotland in the autumn of* 1792, Perth, 1793.


# Aviemore, Inverness-shire

You must pass your night at the single house of Aviemore; sleep you cannot expect, it being the worst inn (except King's House) that I met with in Scotland... I chose to breakfast in any manner, rather than at the dirty inn of Aviemore... No sooner had I put my foot within the walls of that horrible house, than my heart sunk; and I was glad to escape from its stink and smoke very early the next morning.

MURRAY, S, *A Companion and Useful Guide to the Beauties of Scotland*, London, 1799.

Came to Aviemore, but, it hurts me to say, I found the inn I now put up at differing from those I had passed, it being but very indifferently kept: the rooms were dirty.

THORNTON, T, *A Sporting Tour through the Northern parts of England and great part of the Highlands of Scotland*.
London, 1804.

# Ayr, Ayrshire

At present like an old beauty, it shows the ruins of a good face; but is also apparently not only decayed and declined, but decaying and declining every day.

DEFOE, D, *A tour thro' the whole Island of Great Britain*, London, 1727.

The great deduction from the comfort and respectability of Ayr proper is this horrid Newton{a neighbourhood in Ayr}, and the squalid lines of wretched overcrowded hovels, stared out of by unfed and half naked swarms of coal black and seemingly defying inhabitants, that form its eastern approaches.

COCKBURN, H, *Circuit Journeys by the late Lord Cockburn*,
Edinburgh, 1889.

# Badenoch, Inverness-shire

And so indecent are they at funerals, that lately, on the borders of Badenoch, when crossing a bridge, having placed the coffin on the parapet of the bridge to rest themselves, though there were near two hundred of them, it fell over into the water, and was carried down a considerable way, while the friends, relations, and mourners... went along with it, admiring how prettily it sailed... Indeed, as disputes sometimes arise at funerals, it is no uncommon thing to see twenty or thirty men fighting, some on horseback and some on foot, and the corpse laid down on the road, till they see how the fray will end.

HALL, J, *Travels in Scotland by an unusual route*, London, 1807.

# Ballachulish, Argyllshire

Here too I saw, what is not often to be seen now, the waulking of a cloth {waulking is the softening of tweed cloth by soaking it in stale urine and working it with hands or feet}: coming suddenly on the bare legged nymphs in the very orgasm and fury of inspiration, kicking and singing and hallooing as if they had been possessed by twelve devils.

MacCULLOCH, J *The Highlands and Western Isles of Scotland*, London, 1824.

On Loch Leven the take off or toll one has to pay for the permission to enjoy, is - I despair of stating the matter poetically - a downright stench. The nose is mulcted for the pleasures of the eye. If the objects of sight appear to be a heaven, the smells certainly seem to proceed from the other place. This is occasioned by the dirtiness of the fishing villages along the banks of the loch which... have such an ancient and fish like odour, that they actually poison the air half way to Glencoe.

TOWNSHEND, C, *A Descriptive Tour of Scotland*, London, 1840.

We came from Ballachulish, along the shore of Loch Linnhe, this morning, but not so early as we wished... for the people hereabout are intolerably slow both in preparation and in action, and our vehicle (a cart) was long in getting under way, and was long very slowly driven; at one time the driver was actually asleep, and we had to shake him out of his trance.

TOWNSHEND, C, *A Descriptive Tour of Scotland*, London, 1840.

The faces of the people, and particularly of the women and children, would certainly bear a little more water... So long, however, as they are worse housed than their swine, nothing above the habits of swine can be expected.

COCKBURN, H, *Circuit Journeys by the late Lord Cockburn*, Edinburgh, 1889.

# Ballantrae, Ayrshire

The dwelling houses in the village, are, most of them paltry huts. It has been long notable as a nest of smugglers.

HERON, R, *Observations made in a journey through the Western Counties of Scotland in the autumn of 1792*, Perth, 1793.

# Ballindalloch, Banffshire

But for an inn, though I am not very easily distressed with bad accommodations... I never in my life saw a one as this; it is really a perfect burlesque on the name: - a house with rooms, indeed, but no windows. I fancy the people, from their extreme poverty, had taken them out... to save Mr Pitt's additional duty {window tax}... I did not expect a sumptuous bill of fare... but I hoped to find eggs: however, they had none. I was thirsty; I asked for porter – they had none; for brandy – they had none; for rum – they had none... However, I expected that my horses would fare pretty well... but hay – they had none: that, I thought, might be obviated, by a double portion of corn; but alas!– they had none.

THORNTON, T, *A Sporting Tour through the Northern parts of England and great part of the Highlands of Scotland*. London, 1804.

# Banavie, Fort William, Inverness-shire

As the steam boat for Inverness set out from Banavie... we were obliged to sleep at the inn there... beds were at a premium. We were obliged to be content with what the landlord facetiously called 'the barracks,' an out building of small rooms, in each of which four beds were boxed off against the wall. A more uncomfortable night I think I never passed.

PEDESTRIAN, *A six weeks' tour in the Highlands of Scotland*, London, 1851.

# Banff, Banffshire

The poor people in all the western part of it, are still living in miserable huts.

PENNANT, T, *A Tour in Scotland 1769*, London, 1771.

And here I cannot help mention the sagacity of some species of rats, to be found in the Highlands, and which there, as in other parts of Scotland, proceed from one district to another, not by the exercise of their feet, but by adhering to the tails of the horses.

HALL, J, *Travels in Scotland by an unusual route*, London, 1807.

Banff looks inviting at a distance; but, on entering it, the stranger wonders what has become of the smiling city that captivated him from the other side of the river.

SUTHERLAND, A, *A Summer Ramble in the North Highlands*, Edinburgh, 1825.

# Bankfoot, Perthshire

We... stopped at the New Inn, about seven miles from Dunkeld, in hopes of getting some refreshment; and the hostess, a dirty, disagreeable young woman, pitted with the small pox, brought us some wash, she called it broth, which Cowan himself allowed that a pig would not have drunken.

BRISTED, J, *A Pedestrian Tour through part of the Highlands of Scotland in 1801*, London, 1803.

# Beattock, Moffat, Dumfriesshire

This inn was built on a public view by a tax... But Sawney is not an inn-keeping animal. Civility, tidiness, and activity without bustle, are no parts of his nature. The landlord here is a living dunghill.

COCKBURN, H, *Circuit Journeys by the late Lord Cockburn*, Edinburgh, 1889.

# Beauly, Inverness-shire

We had very good wine, but did not drink much of it; but one thing I should have told you was intolerable, viz. the number of Highlanders that attended at table, whose feet and foul linen, or woollen, I don't know which, were more than a match for the odour of the dishes.

BURT, E & JAMIESON, R, *Letters from a Gentleman in the North of Scotland to his friend in London*, London, 1818.

A handsome new bridge renders easy the access to the miserable town of Beauly.

MacCULLOCH, J *The Highlands and Western Isles of Scotland*, London, 1824.

Nothing proves how little the beauties of Scotland are explored more obviously than the entire want of horses, accommodation, or comfort of any kind in a village like Beauly. The inn is little better than an ale house, with no 'entertainment' that we could see, fit for either man or horse.

SINCLAIR, C, *Scotland and the Scotch*, New York, 1840.

# Benbecula, Outer Hebrides

A dreary level of dark peat moss and sodden morass... There is small temptation to linger here, so you hurry on to try and save the next ford, and so reach South Uist.

GORDON-CUMMING, C, *From the Hebrides to the Himalayas*, London, 1876.

# Ben Nevis, Fort William, Inverness-shire

Ben Nevis is redolent of tourists. The path up it is a perfect
turnpike road, where Mrs Dip, the chandler's wife from
Glasgow, parasol in hand, overwhelms with her bulk, some
poor little sheltie (mountain pony), of which you can only see
the head and tail; and greasy citizens lard the lean earth as
they puff along after their guides, and cast impatient glances
at the provision baskets they carry, prescient of ham, chicken,
sausages and ginger-pop.

TOWNSHEND, C, *A Descriptive Tour of Scotland*, London, 1840.

# Bettyhill, Sutherland

The hovels of the peasants near Bettyhill are
extremely rude, and their occupants appeared to be
far from prosperous.

WELD, C, *Two months in the Highlands, Orcadia, and Skye*,
London, 1860.

# Black Isle, Ross and Cromarty

The yeast in Inverness is obtained from the smugglers who
make whisky in the Black Isle; that yeast is thought better
than any other.

SOUTHEY, R, *Journal of a tour in Scotland in 1819*,
London, 1929.

# Blackmount/Rannoch Moor, Argyllshire

If no one would willingly go to Tyndrum a second time, or remain there an hour, so, no one will, from choice, take the road from this point to the King's house and Glencoe, which is dreary in the extreme.

MacCULLOCH, J *The Highlands and Western Isles of Scotland*, London, 1824.

# Blair Atholl, Perthshire

Here we saw a coarse large boned woman washing some sheets in the stream: she had tucked up her petticoats and fastened them around the middle of her body, and with her naked feet was treading and stamping vehemently on the linen. This is a method of washing, which I found to prevail pretty generally in Caledonia, both in the High and the Lowlands. I have seen them practice this elegant mode of exhibiting parts, which civilized nations are, generally, in the habit of imagining it necessary to conceal from public view, at the Leith water... and in many other places... We saw three women in one tub, rivalling Eve in simplicity of nakedness from the waist downwards, and washing linen with their feet, all in glee and merriment.

BRISTED, J, *A Pedestrian Tour through part of the Highlands of Scotland in 1801*, London, 1803.

The two penny, as they call it, is their common ale... This liquor is disagreeable to those who are not used to it... This drink is of itself apt to give a diarrhoea, and therefore, when the natives drink plentifully of it, they interlace it with brandy or whisky.

BURT, E & JAMIESON, R, *Letters from a Gentleman in the North of Scotland to his friend in London*, London, 1818.

Near to it is the castle of Blair, a clumsy white-washed building, more like a cotton manufactory than a nobleman's mansion.

PEDESTRIAN, *A six weeks' tour in the Highlands of Scotland*, London, 1851.

The ducal monster being in London, George and I dared to walk to his castle. Outside - which is all we saw - it is all in a wretched condition, - mean, comfortless, squalid.

COCKBURN, H, *Circuit Journeys by the late Lord Cockburn*, Edinburgh, 1889.

# Braemar, Aberdeenshire

The men are thin, but strong; idle and lazy, except employed in the chase, or anything that looks like amusement; are content with their hard fare, and will not exert themselves farther than to get what they deem necessaries. The common women are in general most remarkable plain; and soon acquire an old look, and by being much exposed to the weather... such a grin, and contraction of the muscles, as hardens greatly their natural hardness of features. I never saw such plainness among the lower rank of females: but the ne plus ultra of hard features is not found till you arrive among the fish women of Aberdeen.

PENNANT, T, *A Tour in Scotland 1769*, London, 1771.

Of the road into Braemar, there is little or nothing to be said; as it is one uniform scene of wildness and desertion, with little character of any kind, and with nothing to vary its wearisome prolongation.

MacCULLOCH, J *The Highlands and Western Isles of Scotland*, London, 1824.

It is still a pleasure to find a female attendant in these Highland inns, instead of the clumsy, half sober, half dressed, male Highland animal who affects the manners of a Bath waiter.

MacCULLOCH, J *The Highlands and Western Isles of Scotland*, London, 1824.

# Brechin, Angus

The approach to Brechin from the north side is rendered disgusting by innumerable carcasses of old horses, which the shoemakers and saddlers of Brechin, the most numerous class of the trades people, purchase for the sake of their skins.

HALL, J, *Travels in Scotland by an unusual route*, London, 1807.

# Bressay, Shetland

The only ferry boat we could procure was a miserable skiff... the two boatmen afforded us a remarkable instance of stupid apathy... we observed that one of the boatmen was not tugging at his oar half so busily as the other, and consequently that the boat was turning to the one side: upon remonstrating with the sluggish ferryman, he, instead of quickening his motions, made a full pause, and hung on his oar gaping with surprise: the other, meanwhile, continued tugging away as hard as ever, nor did he observe what he was doing till he was most alarmed by the boat wheeling about, and almost completing a circle.

NEILL, P, *A Tour through some of the islands of Orkney and Shetland*, Edinburgh, 1806.

# Bridge of Orchy, Argyllshire
## Inveroran Inn

The butter not eatable, the barley cakes fusty, the oat bread so hard I could not chew it, and there were only four eggs in the house, which they had boiled as hard as stones.

WORDSWORTH, D, *Recollections of a tour made in Scotland A.D.* 1803. Edinburgh, 1875.

Lord Breadalbane is building a new inn at Inveroran, upon a poor mean scale, in a situation where a tolerable one would be very useful; but it will be better than the present, which is a wretched hovel, having two beds, the only ones for travellers, in the only sitting room.

SOUTHEY, R, *Journal of a tour in Scotland in* 1819, London, 1929.

# Brownhill, Dumfriesshire

Here we were first honoured with the agreeable attendance of a bare footed female. The accommodations of this place gave us but unfavourable ideas of what we were to experience, particularly in the lodging way. The beds, composed of hard materials, were fixed in large recesses in the wall, by which economy one curtain serves.

SHAW, S, *A Tour, in* 1787, *from London to the Western Highlands of Scotland*, London, 1788.

It was as pretty a room as a thoroughly dirty one could be...
The servant... was a coarse looking wench, barefoot
and bare legged.

WORDSWORTH, D, *Recollections of a tour made in Scotland*
*A.D.* 1803. Edinburgh, 1875.

# Buckhaven, Fife

A miserable row of cottage-like buildings.
DEFOE, D, *A tour thro' the whole Island of Great Britain*,
London, 1727.

# Burghead, Moray

A small fishing town, dirty and putrescent... You cannot be
long in Burghead without being struck by the wild gypsy-like
appearance of many of the persons you see lounging about.

WELD, C, *Two months in the Highlands, Orcadia, and Skye*,
London, 1860.

# Caithness

In Caithness, where the women carry out the dung in baskets on
their backs, while the men lie lounging about the house, doing
nothing but filling the wicker baskets on the women's backs...
In general, the men and women of Caithness, are but of small
stature, as well as the trees... They are stunted creatures, with a
sharp visage, indicative of both intelligence and want. The lairds

and ladies of Caithness seem social, convivial, gay, and merry, in proportion to the misery of the poor slaves, from whose labour and privations they derive the means of their festivity... One thing peculiar to Caithness: the gentlemen gently pinch the toes of the ladies with their own toes, by way of making love, under the table at dinner or supper.

HALL, J, *Travels in Scotland by an unusual route*, London, 1807.

The country too, at all times wretchedly provided with accommodation for travellers, was now more deploringly destitute than ever, in consequence of the depopulating system pursued on the Sutherland estates.

SUTHERLAND, A, *A Summer Ramble in the North Highlands*, Edinburgh, 1825.

The interior of Caithness may be generally described as a tame monotonous level... At length, the lofty ridges on the confines of Sutherland started into view; and from that moment the landscape underwent a striking and agreeable change.

SUTHERLAND, A, *A Summer Ramble in the North Highlands*, Edinburgh, 1825.

For nowhere are those little animated miracles, gnats or midges, more abundant than here... why every square yard contains a population of millions of these little harpies, that pump the blood out of you with amazing savageness and insatiability.

WELD, C, *Two months in the Highlands, Orcadia, and Skye*, London, 1860.

# Caledonian Canal, Inverness-shire

The construction of the locks is similar to those on the Erie Canal, though in workmanship certainly inferior.

CARTER, N, *Letters from Europe comprising The Journal of a Tour through... Scotland... in 1825*, New York, 1827.

# Callander, Perthshire

All the varnish of this inn is insufficient to varnish its defects: from the stable to the kitchen, and the kitchen to the parlour, and the parlour to the bedroom; wants of all kinds, except of pride and negligence; and of bells, which, the more you ring, the more nobody will come... You may ring the bell forty times in a quarter of an hour, or else for a quarter of an hour at one time: it is pretty much the same.

MacCULLOCH, J *The Highlands and Western Isles of Scotland*, London, 1824.

Callander is a long, ugly, one streeted town.

TOWNSHEND, C, *A Descriptive Tour of Scotland*, London, 1840.

# Campbeltown, Kintyre, Argyllshire

There is a crowd upon the pier... and gathering together of luggage, and a furious raid upon it by a crowd of semi-savage gentlemen of the hybrid fisherman breed... We stand... upon Campbeltown quay, while the customary scramble for our luggage is going on. A stalwart, bare legged woman is the victor, who bodily carries off our bag and baggage to a truck... this specimen of the Highlander's beast of burden (for this is but too generally the character of the women).

BEDE, C, *Glencreggan or, A Highland home in Cantyre*, London, 1861.

# Cape Wrath, Sutherland

The people here are much attached to it, and, like the Laplanders, with regard to their country, think it one of the finest places on the face of the earth; and it is fortunate they think so. Were it not the case, it would soon become a desert. Some of the people along this coast... do not think it a crime, when a ship is wrecked, to carry off valuable articles from it... and when dead men are washed ashore, they who find them first think themselves fortunate, as they have it in their power to rifle their pockets, and secrete the property found on them.

HALL, J, *Travels in Scotland by an unusual route*, London, 1807.

# Carnwath, Lanarkshire

Presently thereafter, a little dirty damsel brought us in a platter of some wash, which she called broth, with two wooden spoons in it... We attempted, but in vain, for our very gorge rose against every mouthful, to swallow the said semi-solid substance.

BRISTED, J, *A Pedestrian Tour through part of the Highlands of Scotland in 1801*, London, 1803.

# Castle Douglas, Kirkcudbrightshire

Gelston. Ugliness itself.

COCKBURN, H, *Circuit Journeys by the late Lord Cockburn,* Edinburgh, 1889.

# Cawdor Castle, Nairnshire

But, O these miserable nobles. The edifice, though pretended to be still maintained as a place of residence, is all in the most humiliating condition of paltry disrepair... The whole castle is in the same scandalous style of bad taste and beggarly penury.

COCKBURN, H, *Circuit Journeys by the late Lord Cockburn,* Edinburgh, 1889.

# Cladich, Loch Awe, Argyllshire

At the village of Cladich we made a short pause, to examine a manufactory of tartan plaids. The show, however, was small, and the inhabitants seem not to have been enriched by the reputation of their fabrics; for it is a mean and dirty place.

CARTER, N, *Letters from Europe comprising The Journal of a Tour through... Scotland... in 1825,* New York, 1827.

# Coupar Angus, Perthshire

A small village with a very bad public house.

THOMSON, W, *Tour in England and Scotland in 1785*, London, 1788.

A poor town, very unlike, both in appearance and prosperity, to its namesake of Fife.

BOTFIELD, B, *Journal of a Tour Through the Highlands of Scotland during the Summer of 1829*, Edinburgh, 1830.

# Crawfordjohn, Lanarkshire

A small poor village of two or three houses, and a poor church... The church indeed is of somewhat better building than the houses, but such a one in most parts of England would be taken for a barn... Most of the men, especially the meaner sort, wear thumb caps in Scotland, which they call bonnets.

LONDONER, *North of England and Scotland in 1704*, Edinburgh, 1818.

# Creagan, Argyllshire

We sought shelter and refreshment at the first habitation we came to, which proved to be a little roadside public house of two rooms, with a thatched roof. On entering I addressed the mistress of the establishment, saying, we had got sadly wet and wished to get our clothes dried by the fire; but she only remarked there 'was na muckle on't,' and continued her previous occupation without offering any assistance or expressing any commiseration at our uncomfortable plight. We were annoyed, and could not help thinking, how different it would have been in an English cottage of the same grade – the whole family would have been in a bustle to accommodate us; dry clothes, the best they had, would have been offered... It is the opinion of many... that the Gaelic language will never be eradicated from the Highlands; as, to use the emphatic words of a gentleman with whom we conversed on the subject, the 'children sucked it in with their mother's milk.' The woman, of whom we have just spoken, had a family of four or five children, and none of them understood a word of English.

PEDESTRIAN, *A six weeks' tour in the Highlands of Scotland*, London, 1851.

## Creetown, Wigtownshire

Beautifully situated, and seen at a little distance amidst their sheltering trees, look like capitals in Arcadia; but oh, oh! When they are entered. Not even the peat flavoured air... can save them. Sties for human swine.

COCKBURN, H, *Circuit Journeys by the late Lord Cockburn*, Edinburgh, 1889.

## Crianlarich, Perthshire

At Cree in La Roche (sic), we dined, or rather attempted it; and Mr Garrard, from the meanness of the inn, had really rode past it... Uncomfortable as the house was, we found good eggs, fresh barley bannocks, and tolerable porter.

THORNTON, T, *A Sporting Tour through the Northern parts of England and great part of the Highlands of Scotland*. London, 1804.

# Cromarty, Ross and Cromarty

We intended leaving Cromarty at an early hour; but nine o'clock had chimed before we were able to rouse the lazy ferrymen... The boat grounded on a bank at some distance from the shore; and we were preparing to wade to the beach, when, at a signal from our steersman, a sturdy woman who was waiting our arrival, threw off a fish creel she had on her shoulders, kilted up her tattered robe to a ludicrous degree, and dashing in to the water, carried us, one by one, on her back through the surf.

SUTHERLAND, A, *A Summer Ramble in the North Highlands*, Edinburgh, 1825.

# Crossford, Lanarkshire

We came at length... to a public house on the road; we entered and saw, in a very nasty room... two young females. We asked if we could be provided with some supper and a lodging; the wenches answered No; that we might go on to Lanark, about five miles farther on the road. From a neighbouring apartment, stalked into the place where we were, a tall elderly man, with a very short dirty shirt on, and a red greasy worsted nightcap on his pate; other clothes he had none. He... heard our request for a lodging... while he stood with his back to the two girls, his daughters, scratching his naked posteriors for their edification, for he had elevated the scanty portion of his shirt for the purpose of more easily applying his nails to the part affected. He then turned round to the girls, by which movement he favoured us with the aforesaid exhibition a tergo... and bade them instantly... make up a bed for us in his own room.

We went into a very damp bed in the most filthy chamber imaginable, and swarming with bugs, whereby I was speedily so much bitten that I was in such an intolerable state of irritation as not to endure any longer an abode in bed.

BRISTED, J, *A Pedestrian Tour through part of the Highlands of Scotland in 1801*, London, 1803.

# Cullen, Banffshire

Is a small poor town, without one good house in it.

THOMSON, W, *Tour in England and Scotland in 1785*, London, 1788.

At the fisher town of Cullen, I found an immense number of curs. Upon inquiring the reason of their having so many dogs, I was told they breed them for their skins, which being sewed and blown up like bladders, are fixed by the fishers to their lines, with hooks, to prevent them from sinking.

HALL, J, *Travels in Scotland by an unusual route*, London, 1807.

It is a mean, insignificant place, with some pretensions to antiquity.

SUTHERLAND, A, *A Summer Ramble in the North Highlands*, Edinburgh, 1825.

# Dalkeith, Midlothian

A dirty, shabby place.

MURRAY, S, *A Companion and Useful Guide to the Beauties of Scotland*,
London, 1799.

The houses are generally mean and dirty.

CARR, J, *Caledonian Sketches or A Tour through Scotland in* 1807,
London, 1809.

# Dalmally, Argyllshire
## Dalmally Inn

Dalmally is just the sort of inn where you pay dear for a little,
just because they exhibit a list of wines over the chimney piece,
including champagne or bottled gooseberry... it always raises
my bile to find an inn of this sort of pretension, a vile mixture
of show and parsimony.

TOWNSHEND, C, *A Descriptive Tour of Scotland*, London, 1840.

# Dalwhinnie, Inverness-shire

No one will ever wish to enter Dalwhinnie a second time;
and no one who has crossed its hideous, cold, desolate,
naked, starved, melancholy, moors, will ever willingly
cross them again.

MacCULLOCH, J *The Highlands and Western Isles of Scotland*,
London, 1824.

But let the luckless traveller beware of the lonely inn
at Dalwhinnie, after the shooting season has set in;
for there he will find, as we did, both the house and
the attention of the landlord taken up by parties of
sportsmen... we were but coach company, and what could
we expect but to be crammed in amongst herring eating,
whisky drinking revellers.

TOWNSHEND, C, *A Descriptive Tour of Scotland*, London, 1840.

# Dingwall, Ross and Cromarty

Was in the neighbourhood informed of other singular customs
of the Highlanders. On New Year's Day they burn juniper
before their cattle, and on the first Monday in every quarter
sprinkle them with urine.

PENNANT, T, *A Tour in Scotland* 1769, London, 1771.

A dirty old town.

BOTFIELD, B, *Journal of a Tour Through the Highlands of Scotland during
the Summer of* 1829, Edinburgh, 1830.

Dingwall, the capital of Ross-shire... is a vile place.

SOUTHEY, R, *Journal of a tour in Scotland in* 1819, London, 1929.

# Dollar, Clackmannanshire

The woeful town.

MURRAY, S, *A Companion and Useful Guide to the Beauties of Scotland*,
London, 1799.

# Dornie, Ross and Cromarty

We... reached Dornie Ferry, where, with one honourable exception (and he was an American), we found every man connected with the ferry hopelessly drunk... Some were surly; some were cheery; others helplessly imbecile... When we had waited fully a couple of hours, our American friend thought some of his men might be made to work; and though they presented the lively appearance of inebriated owls, they made a start; and under pressure of startlingly strong language, did succeed in getting across.

GORDON-CUMMING, C, *From the Hebrides to the Himalayas*, London, 1876.

# Dornoch, Sutherland

A small town, half in ruins.

PENNANT, T, *A Tour in Scotland* 1769, London, 1771.

Dornoch, though the chief town of the shire, and a royal burgh, is as paltry a place as may well be conceived; a desolate village situated among arid hillocks of sand, piled up by the sea blast.

SUTHERLAND, A, *A Summer Ramble in the North Highlands*, Edinburgh, 1825.

Dornoch, though one of the meanest of the royal burghs of Scotland, is, nevertheless, the county town of Sutherland.

BOTFIELD, B, *Journal of a Tour Through the Highlands of Scotland during the Summer of* 1829, Edinburgh, 1830.

The Tainites entertain a great contempt for Dornoch, the capital of Sutherland, which is on the opposite side of the bay. The landlord said that as for himself he would not set his foot in such a place: and indeed Mitchell assures us that it is a most miserable place.

SOUTHEY, R, *Journal of a tour in Scotland in* 1819, London, 1929.

# Doune, Perthshire

Doune is a small, ugly, thriving place.

SOUTHEY, R, *Journal of a tour in Scotland in* 1819, London, 1929.

# Drumlanrig, Dumfriesshire

We were not so surprised with the height of the mountains, and the barrenness of the country beyond them, as we were with the humour of the people, who are not in this part, by many degrees, so populous, or so polished, as in the other parts of Scotland.

DEFOE, D, *A tour thro' the whole Island of Great Britain*, London, 1727.

# Dumbarton, Dunbartonshire

He led us to a house kept by an acquaintance of his, as beastly a place as ever a pig would wish to be lodged in... For our refreshment we had some tea and bread, very dirty butter, and a greasy fried fish, which set us both a cascading with the utmost vehemence, and nearly extinguished our lives on the spot... We then examined our linen, and found that, to all appearance, the sheets had been more frequently used since their last washing than those with which the venerable dame Pennycook had accommodated us. It was absurd to think of depositing our carcases in contact with such filth... We got not a wink of sleep; for, during the space of more than three hours, we lay in a most miserable state, till the nastiness all around us, and the pent up stagnant vapour of the room, very nearly put us to death by sickness and suffocation.

BRISTED, J, *A Pedestrian Tour through part of the Highlands of Scotland in 1801*, London, 1803.

This excellent undertaking is conducted chiefly by young women; but as far as personal charms are in question, I confess I never was so much disappointed: out of fifty there was scarcely one even tolerable.

THORNTON, T, *A Sporting Tour through the Northern parts of England and great part of the Highlands of Scotland.* London, 1804.

At this castle we likewise noticed a girl, who differed so widely in plumpness of form, and delicacy of features, from those we had lately observed, that we could not resist the curiosity of inquiring whether or not she was a native of Scotland. She told us she had come from the south of England.

MAWMAN, J, *An Excursion to the Highlands of Scotland and the English Lakes*, London, 1805.

The appearance of which, sooth to say, is mean and miserable... My rest at night was utterly broken by the most terrific screams and yells... this went on till four o'clock... and strange fancies came into my head that I must be in the neighbourhood of a madhouse. In the morning, when I asked the waiter the cause of the disturbance, he seemed not a whit surprised. It was but a drunken row he said; a very common occurrence at

Dumbarton... I was glad to mount the coach, and to get into the pure air out of the dirty town.

TOWNSHEND, C, *A Descriptive Tour of Scotland*, London, 1840.

We found to be a small, uninteresting place, with little attraction, save its ancient fortress, and even that fell far short of my expectations.

PEDESTRIAN, *A six weeks' tour in the Highlands of Scotland*, London, 1851.

They put us into a little parlour, dirty, and smelling of liquors, the table uncleaned, and not a chair in its place.

WORDSWORTH, D, *Recollections of a tour made in Scotland A.D.* 1803. Edinburgh, 1875.

# Dumfries, Dumfriesshire

The farm houses are in general, miserable huts, the people very poor, and the lower class of females exceedingly dirty. The old women, frightful enough of themselves, are rendered still more so by their dress, the outer garment being a long dirty cloak...
Between Dumfries and Moffat... there is not a house in which you can find any accommodation that is tolerable.

THOMSON, W, *Tour in England and Scotland in 1785*, London, 1788.

In the midst of the town is their market place, and in the centre of that stands their tollbooth, round about which the rabble sit, that nauseate the air with their tainted breath.

FRANCK, R, *Northern Memoirs calculated for the Meridian of Scotland... writ in the year 1658*, Edinburgh, 1821.

Our public dinner, as it is called (Commercial Hotel) was the worst I ever beheld, even at a circuit. I record it as a dinner of unexampled abomination... Being unwilling to live two days in a wretched Dumfries inn, we left 'The Commercial Hotel' there, yesterday after breakfast.

COCKBURN, H, *Circuit Journeys by the late Lord Cockburn*, Edinburgh, 1889.

# Dunbar, East Lothian

We had many kinds of their most curious dishes, but some of them very oddly cooked up, that it was but few, many of us could eat of; we had also claret and punch in great plenty; but, with all these, they had a table cloth so dirty, that, at other times, I should with great reluctance have wiped my hands on it; the sight of which alone, would have certainly turned many of our stomachs, had we not been greatly fatigued and hungry with travelling.

VOLUNTEER, *A Journey through part of England and Scotland... in the year* 1746, London, 1747.

A very indifferent inn.

MAWMAN, J, *An Excursion to the Highlands of Scotland and the English Lakes*, London, 1805.

This was a fine sunshiny day, and a very hot one, perhaps, as ever was known for the time of year; and as I passed along over several brooks, were women washing their linen after the manner of their country, which I was altogether unacquainted with. Their way was, they put their linen in a tub about knee-high, and put water to it, and got into the tub without shoes or stockings; and so standing upon their linen, and holding up their clothes to their middles, to save them from soap, trod round and round upon the linen till the water was foul, and then poured it out and put in clean, till the linen was so white as they thought fit. At first I wondered at the sight, and thought they would have been ashamed, as I was, and have let down their clothes till I were by; but though some would let them down halfway their thighs, others went round and round, sometimes with one side towards me, and sometimes with another, without letting down their clothes at all, or taking any notice of me; and particularly a couple of young wenches that were washing together, at my coming by, pulled up their clothes the higher, and, when I was by, stood still and fell a-laughing. I was surprised at this, and was resolved to say somewhat to the next I came to, that showed no more modesty than these had done. It happened the next was a sturdy old woman; and the water spattering up, and the sun shining hot on her skin, I told her she would spoil her breeches. And look, your honour, (says she) these are but old ones; they have 2 great holes in them already: (and seeing I had not assurance enough to stand it, cried after me) and do but see how shagged they are: and still, when I was at a further distance, (said she), when you go to England, I must get you to buy me a new pair. So being out of the reach of her thumb and nails, I ventured to look back, and saw her holding up one leg as if she meant to show me what a dismal condition those breeches of hers were in, and still she had something to say. Spoil my breeches, brother (said she). I never dared to say anything to any of them afterwards.

LONDONER, *North of England and Scotland in* 1704, Edinburgh, 1818.

# Dunblane, Perthshire

Dirty Dunblane, let us pass by it... There's nothing eminent but narrow streets, and dirty houses... And as for their housewifery, let that alone; for if you touch it, you sully your fingers. Ale, tobacco, and strong waters, are the staple of the town.

FRANCK, R, *Northern Memoirs calculated for the Meridian of Scotland... writ in the year 1658*, Edinburgh, 1821.

It is a populous, but dirty place, with nothing interesting about it, except the ruins of the large cathedral.

CARTER, N, *Letters from Europe comprising The Journal of a Tour through... Scotland... in 1825*, New York, 1827.

Dunblane, once the seat of Episcopal grandeur, and a flourishing city, is now a small deserted town, without business or manufacture, and has little to attract the notice of strangers.

PEDESTRIAN, *A six weeks' tour in the Highlands of Scotland*, London, 1851.

# Duncansby Head, Caithness

Duncansby Head rises to a considerable altitude, red, square, and ugly. It is called Dungsby in the country... The latter name is likely to be right, with a reference to Huna Inn.

MacCULLOCH, J *The Highlands and Western Isles of Scotland*, London, 1824.

# Dundee, Angus

We found it... an irregular and unpleasant place, in which all the ill smells in the universe seemed contending for a superiority; while its inhabitants, unusually coarse both in their manners and figures, were strangely huddled together in every street... Our inn partook amply of these inconveniences as well as of the dirt particular to the place, and we were happy in making our escape from it, once more to breathe a purer air.

SKRINE, H, *Tours in the north of England and great part of Scotland*, London, 1795.

A great part of Dundee, situated on a morass, is very insalubrious. In Dundee, it has been remarked, there are more dwarfish, decrepit, and deformed people, and fewer that arrive at old age, than in any other town of equal size in Scotland.

HALL, J, *Travels in Scotland by an unusual route*, London, 1807.

Notwithstanding what I had seen at Pitkeathly, I was surprised at the indelicacy of some people at Dundee. In Holland... you see written in Dutch, and other languages... upon elegant doors, fronting the street, cabinet, or a space for retirement, specifying which is for men, and which for women; and lest any mistake should happen there is the figure of a man painted on the door, in a certain attitude; and on that for women the figure of a woman, in a similar one... the women, particularly about the shore of Dundee, are... indelicate; for, in a certain place there, to which people occasionally retire, I saw men and women completely in sight, and so near, that they might easily, and no doubt did converse with one another.

HALL, J, *Travels in Scotland by an unusual route*, London, 1807.

Give me leave to call it deplorable Dundee.

FRANCK, R, *Northern Memoirs calculated for the Meridian of Scotland...
writ in the year* 1658, Edinburgh, 1821.

Their butter but little better than grease we usually grease
cart wheels with.

FRANCK, R, *Northern Memoirs calculated for the Meridian of Scotland...
writ in the year* 1658, Edinburgh, 1821.

Internally it resembles a continental town – that is, the houses
are old, lofty, and dark – and many of the streets gloomy, ill
swept, and infested with pestilent odours.

SUTHERLAND, A, *A Summer Ramble in the North Highlands*,
Edinburgh, 1825.

Dundee, the palace of Scotch blackguardism, unless
perhaps Paisley be entitled to contest this honour with
it... A stink of atrocity, which no moral flushing seems
capable of cleansing.

COCKBURN, H, *Circuit Journeys by the late Lord Cockburn*,
Edinburgh, 1889.

Many neat cottages and houses of a better description, but as
usual filthy women with their hair in papers.

SOUTHEY, R, *Journal of a tour in Scotland in* 1819,
London, 1929.

# Coopers Public House

We sat down to eat, or rather to make a vain attempt to eat
something which the host called hung beef, but which, in

toughness and in taste, might have passed very snugly and without fear of detection for fried leather.

BRISTED, J, *A Pedestrian Tour through part of the Highlands of Scotland in 1801*, London, 1803.

# Dunfermline, Fife

A decayed town.

DEFOE, D, *A tour thro' the whole Island of Great Britain*, London, 1727.

Dunfermline (always meaning the district), very bad.

COCKBURN, H, *Circuit Journeys by the late Lord Cockburn*, Edinburgh, 1889.

# Dunkeld, Perthshire

The smell of the cattle dung (which is generally very thick about the house) and their peat fire, I believe, keeps them in health, but not free from the Itch {scabies}, which is as common as their oatmeal; and their better sort of people are rarely free from this malady, which they seldom mind to cure any other way than by their dumb music (they having their instruments always about them) and when the spirit moves them, which is most frequent, they are very dexterous in playing both with their arms and fingers, nay, their whole bodies would very often move.

VOLUNTEER, *A Journey through part of England and Scotland... in the year* 1746, London, 1747.

Not long thereafter came our Cicerone, who was an underling indeed; for a thing in a human shape, so debased and so degraded, and so cut down into nothing, I never beheld.

BRISTED, J, *A Pedestrian Tour through part of the Highlands of Scotland in 1801*, London, 1803.

After the exterior has been seen, not much remains for admiration.

CARTER, N, *Letters from Europe comprising The Journal of a Tour through... Scotland... in 1825*, New York, 1827.

The interior of the cathedral, thoroughly Scotch, being most beastly. I think it a duty to record another execration against the almost swindling extortion and offensive insensibility of its noble and most contemptible owner. I cannot understand how a duke can degrade himself by such pecuniary exaction, and nauseate the lieges by keeping the cathedral in so loathsome a state.

COCKBURN, H, *Circuit Journeys by the late Lord Cockburn*, Edinburgh, 1889.

# Dunrobin, Sutherland

It is a proof of increasing decency and civilization that the Highland kilt, or male petticoat, is falling into disuse. Upon a soldier or a gentleman it looks well; but with the common people, and especially with boys, it is a filthy, beggarly, indecent garb.

SOUTHEY, R, *Journal of a tour in Scotland in 1819*, London, 1929.

# Durness Bay, Sutherland

Durness Bay is a shallow inlet of considerable extent, and is utterly uninteresting... Faraid Head, its eastern boundary, is equally without beauty.

MacCULLOCH, J *The Highlands and Western Isles of Scotland*, London, 1824.

The people, according to Mrs Ross, are very religiously inclined, with the exception of those who go yearly to the Wick fishery. The girls bring back about £8, but the money is dearly earned, for it appears that they come back terribly demoralized.

WELD, C, *Two months in the Highlands, Orcadia, and Skye*, London, 1860.

# Dysart, Fife

The town, though a royal burgh, is, as I said before of Dunfermline in the full perfection of decay, and is, indeed, a most lamentable object of a miserable, dying Corporation.

DEFOE, D, *A tour thro' the whole Island of Great Britain*, London, 1727.

# East Wemyss, Fife

To East Wemyss we came tired, hungry, and exhausted... the landlady, a very fat and a very dirty woman, on being asked what we could have, said, -some skate. -Any meat? -No...

As we had no choice, and were sorely pressed with hunger, we were very glad to partake of some tolerable skimmed milk, not good rolls, and decent butter, notwithstanding a few hairs and fleas, which were mixed up with it... We were roused from our pleasing reverie occasioned by seeing Wemyss Castle, by two lusty, sun-burnt, nearly naked wenches, bawling out that we might hear the prettiest songs that ever were. We turned aside into an unfrequented green, and, immediately, a very small dirty man, arrayed in Tartan plaid, saluted our ears with a yell more dismal and doleful that we had ever before the misfortune to be tortured with. Not a syllable did we understand but that the drift of the song was to get a bawbie from us.

BRISTED, J, *A Pedestrian Tour through part of the Highlands of Scotland in* 1801, London, 1803.

# Ecclefechan, Dumfriesshire

There is a bad inn, and it is a poor town too.
MURRAY, S, *A Companion and Useful Guide to the Beauties of Scotland*, London, 1799.

# Edinburgh, Midlothian

The houses mount seven or eight stories high, with many families on one floor, one room being sufficient for all occasions, eating, drinking, sleeping, and shit. The most mannerly step but to the door, and nest upon the stairs. I have been in an island where it was difficult to tread without breaking an egg; but to move here, and not murder a t– is next to an impossibility.

KIRKE, T, *A modern account of Scotland being an exact description of the country, and a true character of the people and their manners*, 1679.

On the south side is the Tron Kirk, and a little farther, in the middle of the street the Guard House, where the Town Guard does duty every night. Those are as a guard to keep the public peace of the city; but I cannot but acknowledge that they are not near so good a safeguard to the citizens, against private robberies, as our watchmen in London are; and Edinburgh is not without such fellows as shop-lifters, house-robbers, and pick-pockets, in proportion to the number of people, as much as London itself.

DEFOE, D, *A tour thro' the whole Island of Great Britain*, London, 1727.

It may be observed, that, as the offices of drudgery and labour, that require not any skill, are generally performed in London by Irishmen, and Welsh people of both sexes; so all such inferior departments are filled in Edinburgh by Highlanders.

THOMSON, W, *Tour in England and Scotland in 1785*, London, 1788.

The women are in general handsome till they approach twenty, when much of their beauty vanishes, as they become large and masculine.

SHAW, S, *A Tour, in 1787, from London to the Western Highlands of Scotland*, London, 1788.

We traversed the streets of Edinburgh at 7 in the morning, assailed, on all sides, by the odoriferous perfumes... which graced the public paths: for in Edinburgh, and indeed in most parts of Scotland... they souse down the golden shower, for the benefit of the passer by, from the windows, together with every kind of filthy, and oftentimes of fatal, materials, as soon as, or even before, darkness overspreads the town... It should seem, from their obstinate adherence to this beastly and barbarous custom, that the Scottish are as much enamoured of faecal perfume and of excrementitious odour, as were, some years since, the inhabitants of Madrid.

BRISTED, J, *A Pedestrian Tour through part of the Highlands of Scotland in 1801*, London, 1803.

As we approached Edinburgh, the women, we observed, were more generally without shoes or stockings. It cannot be but obvious to every Englishman that the inferior Scottish women undergo (we make the remark with sorrow) much severer toil, than females of the same condition in England... From their muscular exertions, their constant exposure to the weather, and probably their living chiefly on fish and oaten bread, the lower classes of that sex in Scotland are universally short and brawny, with arid skins and tarnished complexion, without 'lily tincture on the face,' or any pretentions to beauty.

MAWMAN, J, *An Excursion to the Highlands of Scotland and the English Lakes*, London, 1805.

Houses literally heaped one upon another, water scantily supplied, and people not much habituated to cleanliness render it, while it delights the eye, most powerfully offensive to the nostrils of strangers.

MAWMAN, J, *An Excursion to the Highlands of Scotland and the English Lakes*, London, 1805.

There is an indecency of dress and conduct to be met, sometimes, in Edinburgh, as well as elsewhere. The ladies at the opera, and other play houses in London, have many of them not only their bosoms, but also their neck behind almost quite naked, and in this they are too often imitated by the ladies in the north... There are perhaps, not baser characters to be found anywhere than sometimes in Edinburgh.

HALL, J, *Travels in Scotland by an unusual route*, London, 1807.

There are women in Edinburgh who live by the wages of iniquity as well as elsewhere... The hospitals and physicians books in Edinburgh seem to indicate, that though in proportion to the population there are not so many riotous eaters of the flesh {syphilis}, there are as many viciously inclined people in Edinburgh as in London... It is unfortunate that the police of modern times cannot prevent low ribaldry and abominable language from being used in the streets... One half of the inhabitants of Edinburgh, as well as of Perth, Stirling, and many other towns in Scotland, are evidently originally from the Highlands: and, in general, all the drudgery and severe labour is performed by people from these places, who are generally stout and well made.

HALL, J, *Travels in Scotland by an unusual route*, London, 1807.

At the house of a Scottish clergyman... I happened to mention that I had never yet met with the haggis in Scotland... This singular compound is boiled and brought to the table without being stripped of its envelope; it is cut into slices, like pudding, and eaten without any addition. Its taste is fat and heavy, nor did I feel any regret that the haggis was not an American dish.

SILLIMAN, B, *A Journal of Travels in England, Holland and Scotland... in the years 1805 and 1806*, New York, 1810.

The birth of the New Year is celebrated in this town, with some ceremonies that are peculiar, I believe, to Edinburgh... I was almost a stranger to sleep last night, for the clock had no sooner struck twelve, then crowds of people began to parade the streets, and kept up an incessant noise till morning; there was such tumultuous movements and loud vociferation, that one might have supposed the city had been stormed. It seems that it is the custom to give dinners on the last day of December... and the moment the New Year begins such of the guests as are more fond of high sport, than of decent manners and seasonable sleep, sally out, to celebrate the joyful event. Their heads are half turned with wine, and the mob in the streets, stimulated with whisky, and ripe for deeds of brilliancy, are ready to follow or even to anticipate their example... The civilities of the night are particularly directed to the other sex, and every lady whom too presumptuous curiosity or accident has brought into the streets, is sure to receive the salutation of lips, still humid with the juice of the grape.

SILLIMAN, B, *A Journal of Travels in England, Holland and Scotland... in the years 1805 and 1806*, New York, 1810.

As I was this morning walking in the New Town, I fell in with a military spectacle of some magnitude... Both here and in London, considerable numbers of Highlanders are to be seen who adhere fully to the indecorous and uncomfortable dress of their country. It consists of a plaid cap, a kilt, which is a kind of short petticoat, and a plaid or cloak... They wear also plaid hose reaching halfway up the leg; but even now, in the depth of winter, they have no other covering on the limbs.

SILLIMAN, B, *A Journal of Travels in England, Holland and Scotland... in the years 1805 and 1806*, New York, 1810.

SCOTLAND THE WORST

Is very populous, and has abundance of poor people in it, so that the streets are crowded with beggars.

LONDONER, *North of England and Scotland in 1704*, Edinburgh, 1818.

On the west end of this town is a large castle on a steep stone rock... At the entrance into it is placed a vast large gun they call Mons Meg, and is so large that they say that a tinker got his girl with child in it.

LONDONER, *North of England and Scotland in 1704*, Edinburgh, 1818.

An English gentleman, in his way hither, had some butter set before him in which were a great number of hairs; whereupon, he called to the landlady, desiring she would bring him some butter upon one plate and the hairs upon another, and he would mix them himself.

BURT, E & JAMIESON, R, *Letters from a Gentleman in the North of Scotland to his friend in London*, London, 1818.

Being a stranger, I was invited to sup at a tavern. The cook was too filthy an object to be described; only another English gentleman whispered me and said, he believed, if the fellow was to be thrown against the wall, he would stick to it... We... were very merry till the clock struck ten, the hour when everybody is at liberty... to throw their filth out at the windows... Well, I escaped all the danger, and arrived, not only safe and sound, but sweet and clean, at my new quarters; but when I was in bed I was forced to hide my head between the sheets; for the smell of the filth, thrown out by the neighbours... came pouring into the room to such a degree, I was almost poisoned with the stench.

BURT, E & JAMIESON, R, *Letters from a Gentleman in the North of Scotland to his friend in London*, London, 1818.

Having occasion the next morning... to inquire for a person with whom I had some concerns, I was amazed at the length and gibberish of a direction given me to find him.

BURT, E & JAMIESON, R, *Letters from a Gentleman in the North of Scotland to his friend in London*, London, 1818.

The New Town of Edinburgh is beautifully monotonous, and magnificently dull.

JOHNSON, J, *The Recess or Autumnal relaxations in the Highlands and Lowlands*, London, 1834.

Although cholera has proved itself to be one of the best scavengers that ever visited Europe, yet he left a good deal of work undone in Auld Reekie.

JOHNSON, J, *The Recess or Autumnal relaxations in the Highlands and Lowlands*, London, 1834.

There was, even amongst the well educated, a slight Scotch accent, while amongst the lower orders it became stronger and stronger through many shades almost up to perfect unintelligibility.

MCLELLAN, H, *Journal of a Residence in Scotland*, Boston, 1834.

Thought the ladies strikingly plain, when compared with those of America. The Scotch ladies are too tall, their features too strong and fixed, and their motions constrained. There is not that gracefulness of person, variety of expression, and liveliness of thought that distinguish our own.

MCLELLAN, H, *Journal of a Residence in Scotland*, Boston, 1834.

A set of quadrilles was got up, which only served to confirm my opinion of the dancing of the Scotch. They are very awkward dancers. They move with great exertion, passing through all the steps with awful precision, and distressing gravity.

MCLELLAN, H, *Journal of a Residence in Scotland*, Boston, 1834.

Nowhere have I found the poor cleanly, for comfortable circumstances alone gives a love of order and cleanliness. Even in England, a greater amount of comfortable circumstances is requisite to induce a love of order – I may add, of cleanliness and frugality likewise. But the English poor are too often spendthrifts, drunkards, and buried in dirt. I believe this is still more the case with the Scottish poor. One must think of the filthiness, the stench, the dirt, that one has to inhale in these closes.

KOHL, J, *Travels in Scotland*, London, 1849.

Its very slums are picturesque, and highly agreeable to the pictorial mind, even when most offensive to the moral and physical sense.

BEDE, C, *A Tour in Tartan-Land*, London, 1863.

Well may Edinburgh be called Auld Reekie! and the houses stand so one upon another, that none of the smoke wastes itself upon the desert air before the inhabitants have derived all the advantages of its odour and its smuts. You might smoke bacon by hanging it out of the window... The Wynds, down which an English eye may look, but into which no English nose would willingly venture, for stinks older than the Union are to be found here.

SOUTHEY, R, *Journal of a tour in Scotland in* 1819, London, 1929.

Went to the Orphan Hospital... Shoes and stockings may be worn or not, at the will of the individual, and many of the girls availed themselves of this privilege to go barefoot, wisely accustoming themselves to the hardy and parsimonious, but filthy custom of their countrywomen. The children in general are so handsome that one wonders at the awful ugliness of the men and women. It is the same in France, the Scotch and the French being undoubtedly the two ugliest nations in Europe.

SOUTHEY, R, *Journal of a tour in Scotland in* 1819, London, 1929.

# Canongate

In this part of the street, though otherwise not so well inhabited as the city itself, are several very magnificent houses of the nobility, built for their residence when the court was here. Besides these, there is vast numbers of bawdy houses in this street; which amongst the frequenters of, it is a common question to ask, if they have got a pair of Canon Gate breeches, meaning the venereal distemper, which rages here, as well as in other places... Edinburgh... is certainly a fine city... notwithstanding, it has its faults, and those very great, meaning its nastiness, which is composed of excrements in all parts of the town; and in a morning, about seven o'clock, before the excrements are swept away from the doors, its stinks intolerably, for which, I believe, it exceeds all parts of the world: for after ten o'clock in the evening, it is fortune favours you if a chamber pot, with excrements &c is

not thrown on your head, if you are walking the st
then not a little diversion to a stranger, to hear all pa.
cry out with a loud voice, sufficient to reach the tops of the
houses,...hoad yare hoandie – hold your hand, and means,
do not throw till I am past... When you ascend their stair
cases, which are all stone, the first thing at every landing
presented to your view, are human excrements, one upon
another, and so thick laid, that it is with difficulty you can
pass them without bruising them, which at the same time
emits a most volatile smell, not at all agreeable to strangers.
They keep close-stools in their bedrooms, which they call
boxes, which are emptied out of the windows in the night,
so shitten-luck generally lights on the person who walks at
late hours in the streets.

VOLUNTEER, *A Journey through part of England and Scotland...
in the year* 1746, London, 1747.

I never saw anything like the swarms of children in
Canongate. It may be truly said they are fat, ragged, and
saucy... I was one fine evening walking up this inviting
Canongate, nicely dressed, in white muslin: an arch boy eyed
me, and laid his scheme;- for when I arrived opposite a pool,
in the golden gutter {most likely a euphemism for urine}, in
he dashed a large stone, and like a monkey, ran off chuckling
at his mischief. Though the whole town of Edinburgh is
far more cleanly, in one article, than it used to be, yet the
Canongate still bears strong marks of its old customs; for
'haud yer hand' is still very necessary to cry out; and even
that will not do in the Canongate now, if perchance one
should be there after ten o'clock in the evening; for at that

hour one begins to hear, slop – here, there and everywhere. Even in the middle of the street, where decent folks generally walk for fear of accidents, they are not exempt from splashes... At times one's nose recalls to the mind Sawney's soliloquy on coming within the distance of twenty miles of the capital of Scotland, when he exclaimed, 'ah, canny Edinburgh, I smell you now.'

MURRAY, S, *A Companion and Useful Guide to the Beauties of Scotland*, London, 1799.

I was struck with the palace of the present Duke of Queensberry having been converted into, and now used as, a venereal hospital.

CARR, J, *Caledonian Sketches or A Tour through Scotland in 1807*, London, 1809.

I walked slowly, in the middle of a working day, from the Castle to the Canongate, and I counted four hundred and seventy individuals (men, women, and children) completely idle – most of them taking snuff, and some of them whisky. Let any one walk from St James's Palace to Leadenhall Street, along Pall Mall, the Strand, Fleet Street, Ludgate Hill, Cheapside, and Cornhill – and he will not detect twenty idlers, in all that stupendous tide of human existence. In the evening... I perambulated the streets... for two or three hours. It seemed as if all the wynds, closes,— nay, the beds of sickness had disgorged their tenants!— I sometimes thought the graves had given up their dead; for never, in my life, did I see such a multitude of meagre, stunted, half starved, pallid, and sickly human beings, crowding the street... I do not think the inferior classes of the Scotch are so very industrious as the world imagines... they have not the energetic activity of the Irish, nor the plodding, herculean labour of the English.

JOHNSON, J, *The Recess or Autumnal relaxations in the Highlands and Lowlands*, London, 1834.

## Calton Hill

But as that hill is the common, daily, and nightly lounge of all the vagabonds and loose tribe of the town, the walk over it must be taken with a gentleman in company, else women of any description will be insulted.

MURRAY, S, *A Companion and Useful Guide to the Beauties of Scotland*, London, 1799.

To the north of it is the famous ruin called the 'National Monument,' a disgrace to the inhabitants of the city; and a wooden building called Short's observatory. We were attacked as soon as we reached the top of the hill by an out runner from the latter establishment... A fee of one shilling gained us the sight of some magnified fleas, maggots, and some drops of water, and though last not least a camera obscura view of the neighbourhood.

PEDESTRIAN, *A six weeks' tour in the Highlands of Scotland*, London, 1851.

## Holyrood Palace

Its situation is low, in the oldest and filthiest part of the town. If it possessed any elegance, it could not be seen to advantage, on account of the surrounding buildings... In the Palace itself there is very little worth seeing – certainly nothing to compensate the visitant for the exorbitant expense of passing through the hands of six or eight separate guides, who understand the division of labour, and the art of securing fees.

CARTER, N, *Letters from Europe comprising The Journal of a Tour through... Scotland... in 1825*, New York, 1827.

## Edinburgh High School

The edifice, rooms, and accommodations are in all respects inferior to the institutions of the same kind in New York.

CARTER, N, *Letters from Europe comprising The Journal of a Tour through... Scotland... in 1825*, New York, 1827.

## Edinburgh University

The university alone seems neglected in the midst of rising splendour of the place, and a miserable collection of mean and ruinous buildings disgrace that seminary which has produced some of the brightest luminaries of the age.

SKRINE, H, *Tours in the north of England and great part of Scotland*, London, 1795.

It is to be hoped, that the very coarse and disgusting behaviour, which has so long disgraced the students of the Scottish universities, will give place to a conduct more becoming, and better calculated to denote civilised and polished human beings.

BRISTED, J, *A Pedestrian Tour through part of the Highlands of Scotland in 1801*, London, 1803.

# Assembly Rooms

Having mentioned to some of my friends my admiration of music, I was promised a rich treat, as the competition of the Scottish pipers was at hand... I was pressingly invited to the rehearsal in the ancient Assembly room... I shall never forget it... A Highland piper entered, in full tartan array, and began to press from the bag of his pipes... sounds so long and horrible, that, to my imagination, they were comparable only to those of the eternally tormented... so wretched is this instrument to my ears... each sound being to me equally depressive, discordant, and horrible... The dismal drone of the pipes, which Butler has so well and wittily described:

Then bagpipes of the loudest drones,
With snuffling broken winded tones,
Whose blasts of air, in pockets shut,
Sound filthier than from the gut,
And made a viler noise than swine,
In windy weather when they whine.

As a warlike instrument, the bagpipe may be useful in the field of battle, for its sounds are calculated to scare and annoy. The bagpipe is amongst the very few remaining barbarisms of Scotland.

CARR, J, *Caledonian Sketches or A Tour through Scotland in* 1807, London, 1809.


# Adelphi Theatre

Judging from what we saw this evening, I cannot think the taste of an Edinburgh audience very refined; anything beautiful in sentiment, or sublime in imagination... was passed over with gloomy silence; whilst a stupid joke, or broad grin, which required little stretch of the intellect to appreciate, was received with 'bravo,' 'excellent,' and rounds of applause.

PEDESTRIAN, *A six weeks' tour in the Highlands of Scotland*, London, 1851.

## Theatre Royal

The dancers... wore filibegs, or short petticoats, instead of breeches; and, in the course of their springs and capering, would doubtless have alarmed the sensitive feelings of a member of the Society of the Suppression of Vice, had such a one been present, for the wounded delicacy of the ladies in the pit.

CARR, J, *Caledonian Sketches or A Tour through Scotland in* 1807, London, 1809.

## Newhaven

I must say that, on any point on the wonderfully indented coast of Scotland, there is not one, where a stranger is so much pestered and imposed upon, as at this said Newhaven, by a ragged, ugly, and ill-mannered swarm of tide waiters, such as I have nowhere else, in Scotland, seen.

JOHNSON, J, *The Recess or Autumnal relaxations in the Highlands and Lowlands*, London, 1834.

I saw toiling up the street, and bending under the weight of their heavy creels, some women whom no stretch of the imagination or courtesy could term either beautiful or cleanly... It is true, that Mr Reade says 'After a certain age, the Newhaven fishwife is always a blackguard and ugly.' The Leith and Fisherrow women are inferior to those of Newhaven in comeliness, cleanliness, and respectability... Many of them become 'blackguards', and relapse into drunken, worthless characters. The Irish girls and those who usually go up to Edinburgh at night with oysters, are looked upon, even by their own class, as 'a bad lot,' and fail in sobriety and other virtues.

BEDE, C, *A Tour in Tartan-Land*, London, 1863.

# Elgin, Moray

All these towns, Inverness, Nairn, Forres and Elgin, have a very dismal appearance. Nor can they claim the merit of being very clean, and Elgin, in filthiness, exceeds them all.

THOMSON, W, *Tour in England and Scotland in 1785*, London, 1788.

A paltry town.

SKRINE, H, *Tours in the north of England and great part of Scotland*, London, 1795.

At a sale by auction, in Elgin, I was not a little surprised to hear the auctioneer, using gross and low wit, and not only immodest, but extremely immoral expressions; which, however pleasing they might be to low grovelling minds... were a disgrace in a civilised country, and disagreeable, I think I may venture to say, to nine tenths of the females present. I saw several of them blushing at his expressions... Drollery and gentle satire may be permitted in an auctioneer, but immoral and indecent expressions, in a public character, are shameful in the extreme.

HALL, J, *Travels in Scotland by an unusual route*, London, 1807.

The church and the gaol are old and ugly buildings, and both encumber and disfigure the principal street, in the middle of which they stand. There are scarcely any manufactures, and very little trade in the town, which in consequence displays the appearance both of poverty and idleness... The celebrated ruins of its cathedral, to which I hastened as soon as I had finished a rather late dinner at a dirty inn, are the only attractions to a stranger.

CARR, J, *Caledonian Sketches or A Tour through Scotland in 1807*, London, 1809.

Stayed there (bad inn).

COCKBURN, H, *Circuit Journeys by the late Lord Cockburn*, Edinburgh, 1889.

The city has an ancient air, and an appearance of decay about it.

SOUTHEY, R, *Journal of a tour in Scotland in 1819*, London, 1929.


# Ellon, Aberdeenshire

The wretched little town.

SKRINE, H, *Tours in the north of England and great part of Scotland*, London, 1795.


# Elvanfoot, Lanarkshire

Arrive at a miserable cottage, called an inn.

THOMSON, W, *Tour in England and Scotland in 1785*, London, 1788.

The farm houses are not only mean and incommodious, but have their office houses – barn, byre, stable, peat house, so crowded upon them as to render the close or area before the door, a scene of indescribable filth and confusion.

HERON, R, *Observations made in a journey through the Western Counties of Scotland in the autumn of* 1792, Perth, 1793.

A sorry place of two or three houses.

LONDONER, *North of England and Scotland in* 1704, Edinburgh, 1818.

# Eyemouth, Berwickshire

The cookery was so nasty, and also the women, and the town so stinking, human excrements lying everywhere in the streets, that it requires great caution to tread out of them.

VOLUNTEER, *A Journey through part of England and Scotland... in the year* 1746, London, 1747.

Is a great place for smugglers, and probably derived its name (Hotmouth sic) from the quantity of ardent spirits here landed and swallowed.

CARTER, N, *Letters from Europe comprising The Journal of a Tour through... Scotland... in* 1825, New York, 1827.

# Falkirk, Stirlingshire

A large ill built town.

PENNANT, T, *A Tour in Scotland* 1769, London, 1771.

On entering Falkirk, its narrow streets were so crowded by men, women, and children, that, had not booths and bagpipes betokened a fair, we must confess we should have felt some humane apprehensions as to the sanity of the intellect of its inhabitants.

BOTFIELD, B, *Journal of a Tour Through the Highlands of Scotland during the Summer of* 1829, Edinburgh, 1830.

One smartly dressed young woman we saw near Falkirk in the filthy bare-foot fashion of the country, a custom to which nothing could ever reconcile our English feelings.

SOUTHEY, R, *Journal of a tour in Scotland in* 1819, London, 1929.

# Falkland, Fife

Falkland is a mean and obscure village... and boors and weavers are its only inhabitants.

SUTHERLAND, A, *A Summer Ramble in the North Highlands*, Edinburgh, 1825.

# Fife

Indeed our pleasure from viewing the country was much diminished by the contemplation of the penury and misery of the inhabitants; such squalid, wretched, emaciated, rude, inhuman, dejected, lifeless, indolent, spiritless, sluggish beings we had never beheld.

BRISTED, J, *A Pedestrian Tour through part of the Highlands of Scotland in* 1801, London, 1803.

# Fochabers, Moray

A wretched town.

PENNANT, T, *A Tour in Scotland* 1769, London, 1771.

It is astonishing how plain the country women are here:
I did not discover one that was tolerable... and, as many of
them were the daughters of farmers and mechanics who
live decently, I was much at a loss to account for this scanty
distribution of beauty.

THORNTON, T, *A Sporting Tour through the Northern parts of England and great part of the Highlands of Scotland*. London, 1804.

The old town... is an assemblage of miserable huts.

HALL, J, *Travels in Scotland by an unusual route*, London, 1807.

I wasted an hour on Gordon Castle, which I despised so much
when I first saw it, above forty years ago, that I had never taken
the trouble to look at it since, often as I have passed it. I find it as
contemptible as ever.

COCKBURN, H, *Circuit Journeys by the late Lord Cockburn*, Edinburgh, 1889.

# Forfar, Angus

Forfar is a royal burgh of great antiquity, and
of little consequence.

BOTFIELD, B, *Journal of a Tour Through the Highlands of Scotland during the Summer of 1829*, Edinburgh, 1830.

# Forres, Moray

On a moor, about four miles further, Shakespeare places the
encounter of Macbeth and the weird sisters; and it is judiciously
chosen, for all the women in this part of the country have the
appearance of midnight hags. They only want the cauldron and
the broom stick to complete them for the stage.

THOMSON, W, *Tour in England and Scotland in 1785*, London, 1788.

The town stands on a gently raising ground, near the bay
of Findhorn; it is very ancient, gloomy, and dirty. Poverty
seemed to hang over it as an evil spirit. In the street I saw
several squalid figures, who induced me to think that the race
of Macbeth's witches was not quite extinguished.

CARR, J, *Caledonian Sketches or A Tour through Scotland in 1807*,
London, 1809.

The next town is Forres, famous for nothing except for that
infamous vermin the rat... I have been told, that these vermin
politicians storm the town once or twice a year, to the terrifying
amazement of all the inhabitants.

FRANCK, R, *Northern Memoirs calculated for the Meridian of Scotland...
writ in the year 1658*, Edinburgh, 1821.

The moor where Macbeth and Banquo met the weird sisters...
was in our route, about two miles from Forres... No flight of
fancy, however strained, can conjure the dull, listless forms of
the rural peasantry into the brave band of warriors, joyously
returning from a victorious conflict.

PEDESTRIAN, *A six weeks' tour in the Highlands of Scotland*,
London, 1851.

# Fort Augustus, Inverness-shire

Here was also many foot races performed by both sexes, which made many droll scenes. It was necessary to entertain life in this manner; otherwise, by the constant view of mountains surrounding us, we should have been affected with hypochondriacal melancholy.

VOLUNTEER, *A Journey through part of England and Scotland... in the year* 1746, London, 1747.

The climate here was so excessive bad, that we had a winter from the beginning of July... continually raining, and cold winds blowing, which occasioned great numbers to fall sick daily, as well in their minds, as bodies; for it is a rarity to see the sun, but constantly black skies, and rusty looking, rocky mountains, attended with misty rains and cutting winds... The flies and fleas were also a great plague to us in our huts as I have seen them in some very hot countries. Our army is marched away... so I am just a-going to be relieved from this wretched place.

VOLUNTEER, *A Journey through part of England and Scotland... in the year* 1746, London, 1747.

A small village, or rather a collection of wretched huts; and the inn is a truly miserable residence, void of all comfort, and attended with every possible inconvenience.

SKRINE, H, *Tours in the north of England and great part of Scotland*, London, 1795.

Is in a state of great neglect, and appears to be going very fast to decay.

MURRAY, S, *A Companion and Useful Guide to the Beauties of Scotland*, London, 1799.

There are great swarms of little flies which the natives call malhoulakins... these are so very small, that, separately, they are but just perceptible... and, being of a blackish colour, when a number of them settle upon the skin, they make it look as if it was dirty; there they soon bore their little augers into the pores, and change the face from black to red.

BURT, E & JAMIESON, R, *Letters from a Gentleman in the North of Scotland to his friend in London*, London, 1818.

No one will stay an hour at Fort Augustus if he can avoid it.

MacCULLOCH, J *The Highlands and Western Isles of Scotland*, London, 1824.

The village is a poor place; the inn most inconveniently built, and not well situated... Dr Johnson says in one of his letters 'the best night I have had these twenty years was at Fort Augustus.' He therefore remembered the place with pleasure. And so shall I - always excepting the quarters, which could not have been filthier in his time than they are at present.

SOUTHEY, R, *Journal of a tour in Scotland in* 1819, London, 1929.

Our comical host every day exhibited at breakfast the fish which he intended for our dinner... they were cut across like crimped fish, and then broiled, till the flavour, whatever it might have been, was broiled out of them. Moreover, melted butter, which the Scotch use with nothing, except fish, is in Scotland such a vile mixture of flour and butter, that it is not fit to be used with anything.

SOUTHEY, R, *Journal of a tour in Scotland in* 1819, London, 1929.

# Fort William, Inverness-shire

The inns at Maryburgh, the little town close by Fort William, are very bad, and dreadful for horses... The inn kept by a Scotch woman, has, if there be any, the preference in cleanliness, over that kept by an Englishman, but in either inn you will stand in need of your own blankets &c, and eatables too.

MURRAY, S, *A Companion and Useful Guide to the Beauties of Scotland*, London, 1799.

The entrance to the town on Maryburgh, adjoining the fort, has little to gratify the eye... it is a long street of indifferent houses... The inn is rather destitute of accommodation... I passed by several huts, more miserable I think than any I had yet seen, which, from the smoke issuing through the roof, and their squalid appearance, resembled so many reeking dunghills.

CARR, J, *Caledonian Sketches or A Tour through Scotland in* 1807, London, 1809.

I was now in the region of rain, which descended with little intermission, during my stay at Maryburgh, with a copiousness which I have not often beheld. Rain, which continues in this neighbourhood for nine or ten weeks together, is called by the natives by the gentle name of a shower.

CARR, J, *Caledonian Sketches or A Tour through Scotland in* 1807, London, 1809.

In one respect, Fort William possesses the distinguishing marks of a capital: idleness... To Londoners, it may be new to see the single street of which it consists, crowded with idle men walking about with their hands in their pockets, or collected in groups to yawn together or converse on monosyllables; except when roused to louder talk by an occasional sojournment to a whisky house.

MacCULLOCH, J *The Highlands and Western Isles of Scotland,* London, 1824.

There is nothing interesting about the fortress, nor in the dirty little village of Gordonsburgh.

CARTER, N, *Letters from Europe comprising The Journal of a Tour through... Scotland... in 1825,* New York, 1827.

We had a most comfortless arrival at Fort William, where the inn keeper and his aides-de-camp were all unwillingly roused from their sleep to give us admission, and grumblingly opened a door, by which we entered one of the worst inns I ever yet encountered. The windows were without shutters, the beds without curtains, the doors without bolts, the floors without carpets, and the candlesticks without extinguishers. After a short but comfortless sejour at Fort William, we enjoyed the only pleasure that the inn there can afford to travellers, and that is, to get away.

SINCLAIR, C, *Scotland and the Scotch,* New York, 1840.

The town is one long, mean, filthy street; the inn, abominably dirty... This is the only inn in which we have met with dishonesty in wine, Cape having been produced here for Sherry.

SOUTHEY, R, *Journal of a tour in Scotland in 1819,* London, 1929.

# Foyers, Inverness-shire

A very indifferent public house, where we were obliged to dine on very bad fare.

THOMSON, W, *Tour in England and Scotland in 1785*,
London, 1788.

The aspect of the place was wretched, but there was no other house of entertainment in this dreary region; and we were obliged to eat the dinner we had brought... in a room without furniture or ceiling, and open at the roof to every attack of the weather.

SKRINE, H, *Tours in the north of England and great part of Scotland*,
London, 1795.

I believe the Highlanders to be stout men, both in body and mind; and I also know they will dare do many things for whisky: but I cannot well credit what was told me at Fort Augustus of one who, for the trifling wager of a bottle of that spirit, not only put himself into the river at the top of the fall of Foyers, but voluntarily went down the cataract into the pool... and climbed up the rock side, safe and unhurt, saying 'that was nothing to the fall of Niagara.'

MURRAY, S, *A Companion and Useful Guide to the Beauties of Scotland*,
London, 1799.

You would be amused to see what useful people women are in the far north. They drive the carts, hold the ploughs, in short, do all the manual labour, and if a cottager loses his horse, or ox, or any other beast of burden, he marries a wife to make up the difference.

SINCLAIR, C, *Scotland and the Scotch*, New York, 1840.

# Galloway

The inhabitants of Galloway may appear to be, in some
instances, indolent and deficient in inventive ingenuity.

HERON, R, *Observations made in a journey through the Western Counties of
Scotland in the autumn of* 1792, Perth, 1793.

# Garvamore, Laggan,
# Inverness-shire.

A lone house, with which you can have nothing to do but to bait
your horse at, it being a miserable place indeed.

MURRAY, S, *A Companion and Useful Guide to the Beauties of Scotland*,
London, 1799.

# Garve, Ross and Cromarty

The only man who we saw in a kilt during this day's journey
was a poor idiot, who ran after the chaise, not to beg, but with
an idiotic delight at seeing it.

SOUTHEY, R, *Journal of a tour in Scotland in* 1819, London, 1929.

# Gatehouse of Fleet,
# Kirkcudbrightshire

I wish I could honestly add, that the morals of these good people
have been improved with their circumstances. But prostitution
and breaches of chastity have lately become frequent here.
Tippling houses are wonderfully numerous... The licentiousness

of Gatehouse affords frequent business for the neighbouring Justices... Men habitually addicted to drunkenness, and women abandoned to prostitution ought to be invariable discharged from employment, and dismissed out of the village... The use of whisky should be discouraged; and good malt liquors, ale and porter, introduced in its stead.

HERON, R, *Observations made in a journey through the Western Counties of Scotland in the autumn of* 1792, Perth, 1793.

# Girvan, Ayrshire

The houses are huts more miserable than those of Ballantrae. They are so low as to seem, at the south end of the village, rather caves dug in the earth, than houses built upon it... The inn at which we were directed to stop was a most miserable one. We could not obtain accommodation for the night. Hardly could we procure refreshments for ourselves and our horses. Some whisky was brought us which tasted strongly of turpentine; and some pease-bannock too tough to be eaten.

HERON, R, *Observations made in a journey through the Western Counties of Scotland in the autumn of* 1792, Perth, 1793.

# Glasgow, Lanarkshire

Its situation is very fine; but the town is like all other great manufacturing trading towns; with inhabitants very rich, saucy, and wicked.

MURRAY, S, *A Companion and Useful Guide to the Beauties of Scotland*, London, 1799.

I asked a decently dressed elderly man to tell us where we could obtain a lodging. He looked at me for half a minute and... directed us to a goodly looking house. We stopped awhile at the door, and listened to a psalm which was sung by a clear and well toned male voice. We were much pleased at this... I knocked, and a venerable matron presently appeared, and showed us to a tolerably furnished room. She immediately left us without speaking a single word; during her absence we could hear... the same psalm singing voice pray, and read portions of the scripture aloud... Presently came unto us a young damsel, ruddy and plump, with yellow locks, and rather a dirty face, and not dressed altogether so decently as modesty requires; in good truth, she was but very slenderly clad, and looked full wantonly withal. The lady soon give us to understand, that we had staggered into a bagnio {brothel}, and she was ready to amuse us... We sheered out of the house with all due precipitation and velocity, the wench damning us for a couple of pitiful sneaking rascals, that had no spirit.

BRISTED, J, *A Pedestrian Tour through part of the Highlands of Scotland in 1801*, London, 1803.

On one side of the street, almost in every house, I heard psalms singing and fervent prayers... while on the other, there was nothing to be heard but swearing, blaspheming, and the most obscene and abusive language... And it was astonishing to see in some places a set of drunkards and debauchees reeling from the bagnios, and, at others, numbers going leisurely home with their bibles under their arm... The manners of the common people here were never so profligate; and their high wages but serve to furnish them with the means of becoming more wicked; and, owing to the

SCOTLAND THE WORST

mixture of the sexes at the manufactories, infant prostitution is, it seems, not uncommon.

HALL, J, *Travels in Scotland by an unusual route*, London, 1807.

Glasgow appears to have been accidentally built over one of... Vulcan's most extensive smitheries; for, at each second of time, we see towering columns, or wreathing volumes of the densest smoke, belched forth from a thousand infernal lungs, through pipes or tubes of most gigantic altitudes and dimensions. The only place which can rival - or perhaps excel - Glasgow, in this respect, is Bilston, near Birmingham, where the inhabitants inhale more smoke and sulphur than if they lived in the crater of Vesuvius during a smart eruption.

JOHNSON, J, *The Recess or Autumnal relaxations in the Highlands and Lowlands*, London, 1834.

Glasgow contains some very tasteful and elegant building... and though well laid out, falls very far short of Edinburgh, in all that is beautiful and rich.

MCLELLAN, H, *Journal of a Residence in Scotland*, Boston, 1834.

We went a rambling about the town. The street in which our hotel is, had already shown us the best of it. Most of the others are dirty and ill-conditioned and abounding in abominable savours. A drizzle... added neither to their beauty nor their cleanliness.

TOWNSHEND, C, *A Descriptive Tour of Scotland*, London, 1840.

The smoke of Glasgow, arising from its numerous chemical works, is particularly offensive and injurious. I was informed that on this account it was necessary to remove the botanic gardens out of the neighbourhood of the city.

KOHL, J, *Travels in Scotland*, London, 1849.

In the streets, in the neighbourhood of the Cross, the crowds were especially great... The sight of such a mass of people, among whom were whole families of beggars, going up and down, singing their miseries, whilst they were begging their bread at the corner of every street, yielded altogether a most melancholy impression.

KOHL, J, *Travels in Scotland*, London, 1849.

We also thought the manners of the people greatly superior; the inhabitants of modern Athens being noted for their coldness and formality, their hauteur, and unbending etiquette; while the people of Glasgow are remarkable for their kind and hospitable demeanour, unchecked by affectation or unnecessary form.

PEDESTRIAN, *A six weeks' tour in the Highlands of Scotland*, London, 1851.

If the citizens are as saturated with the Darwin theory as they are with the odour of whisky, we might almost expect that, in the course of time, they would be transmuted into whisky bottles.

BEDE, C, *A Tour in Tartan-Land*, London, 1863.

The suburbs of Glasgow extend very far, houses on each side of the highway, - all ugly, and the inhabitants dirty.

WORDSWORTH, D, *Recollections of a tour made in Scotland A.D. 1803*. Edinburgh, 1875.

I also could not but observe a want of cleanliness in the appearance of the lower orders of the people.

WORDSWORTH, D, *Recollections of a tour made in Scotland A.D. 1803*. Edinburgh, 1875.

Of all the judicial spectators in Scotland, those of
Glasgow are the worst. They are the least attentive, and by
far the most vulgar.

COCKBURN, H, *Circuit Journeys by the late Lord Cockburn*,
Edinburgh, 1889.

## Glasgow University

A spirit of liberality and accommodation towards
strangers certainly did not appear to prevail to a very great
degree among the subordinate officers of the university.
The superintendent of the museum was monosyllabic in
his replies to our enquiries, and nothing was seen which
was not paid for.

CARTER, N, *Letters from Europe comprising The Journal of a Tour through...
Scotland... in 1825*, New York, 1827.

Had I not been told what it was, I should certainly have taken it
for a mad-house.

TOWNSHEND, C, *A Descriptive Tour of Scotland*, London, 1840.

## Glasgow Cathedral

The cathedral, to which we next went, is poor when compared
to many of our own.

TOWNSHEND, C, *A Descriptive Tour of Scotland*, London, 1840.

## Glasgow Green

Here the gentlemen resort to their favourite amusement, the
game of golf... It is a wholesome exercise for those who do not
think such gentle sports too trivial for men, being performed

with light sticks and small balls, and is by no means so violent as cricket, trap-ball, or tennis.

THORNTON, T, *A Sporting Tour through the Northern parts of England and great part of the Highlands of Scotland*. London, 1804.

So abandoned are some of the lower orders about Glasgow, that on a Sunday afternoon, in the green... one of the inhabitants, with an abandoned woman, that had agreed to it, while his companions and those forming the ring, continued to shout and applaud him, did what, even cats, elephants, and many other of the inferior animals avoid in public, for a Scotch pint of gin... Generally, after it grew dark, and during the whole night, the worthless part of the inhabitants practiced there every species of impurity and lewdness... I do not pretend to develop the cause; but certainly there seems to be an extraordinary degree of shameless lewdness among the lower classes in Glasgow. The very lowest class, as porters, labourers, watchmen, &c, are for the most part, either Highlanders, or the descendants of Highlanders.

HALL, J, *Travels in Scotland by an unusual route*, London, 1807.

## East End

By the time we have reached this spot, our senses of sight, and hearing, and smell will tell us that Glasgow, like London, has its East as well as its West End... The second city in the kingdom can rival the first in its slums... they are as equally filthy to the outward and moral senses as are the slums of any other great city. The Saltmarket, the Gallowgate, the Cowcaddens, and the Goosedubbs of eastern Glasgow are the very antipodes of... the western parts of the city. Few strangers would wish to penetrate into the inmost recesses of these filthy spots... Dirt and whisky shops reign supreme in every direction, and the character of the people is reduced by them to a very low state of debasement. It is the misfortune of the city that the worst elements of its national character should here be combined with the worst elements of the Irish character.

BEDE, C, *A Tour in Tartan-Land*, London, 1863.

While the nose is assailed with countless stinks, the ear is stormed by a babel of bastard Scotch and bad English, mixed with fragments of genuine Gaelic, and the rolling periods and rough brogue that mark the Irish Celt... At every step there is an inducement held out to you to 'jest to wet yer thrapple;' until a fight between two drunken women drives you from the scene.

BEDE, C, *A Tour in Tartan-Land*, London, 1863.

## Saracen's Head Inn

But with my first pleasant sensations also came the feeling that we were not in an English inn – partly from its half furnished appearance, which is common in Scotland... and partly from the dirtiness of the floors.

WORDSWORTH, D, *Recollections of a tour made in Scotland A.D. 1803*. Edinburgh, 1875.

## Buck's Head Inn

The inns in large cities are generally detestable, and this does not appear to form an exception from the common rule.

SOUTHEY, R, *Journal of a tour in Scotland in* 1819, London, 1929.

# Glenbarr, Kintyre, Argyllshire

It is a subject equally delicate and unsavoury even to hint
at... when I say that there is not a single outbuilding of any
description attached to the school premises, for the use of
either of the inmates or the scholars (and... the cottages are
without such accommodations), I am mentioning a fact
which makes itself known to the tourist in the Highlands in
various disagreeable ways, and which is an evidence of a trait
of national character that is both repulsive and disgusting,
both to the moral and physical senses... The Highland tourist
who wishes to botanise on a dyke side, is therefore strongly
recommended to choose his dyke at a considerable distance
from a human habitation.

BEDE, C, *Glencreggan or, A Highland home in Cantyre*, London, 1861.

# Glencoe, Argyllshire
## King's House Inn

This house is so ill attended to by the old rascal who lives in
it, that there is not a bed fit to sleep in, nor anything to eat,
notwithstanding that he has it rent free. In the morning, leave
this cursed place and ride to Fort William.

THOMSON, W, *Tour in England and Scotland in 1785*,
London, 1788.

You can get nothing but meal and water for your horses...
King's House is a miserable place, fit only for drovers; but
having my chief necessaries with me, I did not much feel
its comfortless state, except from the closeness of the room,
and the intolerable smoke pervading the whole house...

Few beings, but drovers, take up their quarters at this house; not wholly because of its desolate situation, but because it is very dirty. It is one of the houses government provides; therefore, as the folks who keep it have it rent free, it ought to be made more comfortable for travellers... As soon as I had taken my short meal, and secured my pig hole to sleep in, I left my maid to take care of everything, and mounted the cart. {The author visited Glencoe, and returned.} King's House was full of people, and I made my way to my sty through columns of smoke... I soon eat my bit of supper, half choked with smoke, and in danger of getting cold by an open window, the damp from the rain pouring in, and my petticoats tucked to my knees for fear of the dirt, which was half an inch thick on the floor.

MURRAY, S, *A Companion and Useful Guide to the Beauties of Scotland*, London, 1799.

Here provisions were scarce and poor. It is a miserable and dirty hut.

HALL, J, *Travels in Scotland by an unusual route*, London, 1807.

Although the inn has a regal name... its accommodations of course cannot be very good, situate as it is, in a remote and sterile district. The bread on which we dined, with the addition of an egg, was brought from Glasgow... and had been baked perhaps some ten days before. The stable was as scanty as the larder, and it was soon ascertained that no other conveyance could be had than a cart without a seat, and a skeleton white horse, on which an image of starvation and death rode as driver.

CARTER, N, *Letters from Europe comprising The Journal of a Tour through... Scotland... in 1825*, New York, 1827.

The house looked respectable at a distance... but when we came close to it the outside forewarned us of the poverty and misery within... The first thing we saw on entering the door was two sheep hung up, as if just killed from the barren moor, their bones hardly sheafed in flesh. After we had waited a few minutes... a woman, seemingly about forty years old, came to us in a great bustle, screaming in Erse, with the most horrible guinea hen or peacock voice I ever heard, first to one person, than another. She could hardly spare time to show us upstairs, for crowds of men were in the house – drovers, carriers, horsemen, travellers, all of whom she had to provide with supper, and she was as she told us, the only woman there. Never did I see such a miserable, such a wretched place... the floors far dirtier than an ordinary house could be if it were never washed, as dirty as a house after a sale on a rainy day... With length of time... supper came – a shoulder of mutton so hard it was impossible to chew the little flesh that might be scraped off the bones.

WORDSWORTH, D, *Recollections of a tour made in Scotland A.D.* 1803. Edinburgh, 1875.

# Glenfinnan, Inverness-shire

## Glenfinnan Monument

A cake house, without even the merit of containing cakes; and with a tower – tower, is a profanation of such a word, since the whole building resembles a carpenter's mallet with the handle uppermost... It really is very hard upon poor Scotland, that its

money should be thus spent in blotting and deforming its land
with such monstrosities.

MacCULLOCH, J *The Highlands and Western Isles of Scotland*,
London, 1824.

# Glenkens, New Galloway, Kirkcudbrightshire

That of all that part of mankind who earn their maintenance
by their labour, country mechanics and labourers in husbandry
are usually the most intelligent. Their intelligence is not
diminished by their being intermixed among shepherds.

HERON, R, *Observations made in a journey through the Western Counties of
Scotland in the autumn of 1792*, Perth, 1793.

# Glen Moriston, Ross and Cromarty

## Cluanie Inn

We rested that night at the little inn of Cluanie, where on all the
plates at dinner, these words were inscribed, 'Life is short, so
spend it well.' Certainly no one will spend more of it than they can
help here, as the very necessaries of life are luxuries unattainable
on any terms: my bed was a mere hole in the wall, our dinner
consisted of real buttered eggs, with very salt ham, and we had
not even the consolation at being angry at their many deficiencies,
as the poor people were so perfectly civil and well meaning.

SINCLAIR, C, *Scotland and the Scotch*, New York, 1840.

In the midst of the wilderness, twelve miles from Shiel, stands the little inn of Cluanie, where you will find a shake-down and rough fare.

WELD, C, *Two months in the Highlands, Orcadia, and Skye*, London, 1860.

Mere drovers' quarters, and bad quarters for the poorest drovers.

COCKBURN, H, *Circuit Journeys by the late Lord Cockburn*, Edinburgh, 1889.

# Glen Orchy, Argyllshire

The instinctive attachment of the Highlanders to the bagpipe, more than compensates for its deficiencies as an instrument of music... When played in the open air... produces... a pleasing effect; though, on a breezy morning, the portion of this boisterous music we may chance to catch, leaves us no reason to regret that the other half is lost to the ear.

BOTFIELD, B, *Journal of a Tour Through the Highlands of Scotland during the Summer of 1829*, Edinburgh, 1830.

# Grantown on Spey, Moray

After a long, but delightful day's ramble, we reached Grantown, much fatigued. Strangers here appeared to attract a good deal of notice, of which we received a due share; and we asked one person, whose impertinent curiosity annoyed us, if he thought he knew us, when he replied, 'Why, I dinna', but I've known a great many queer folk in my day.'

PEDESTRIAN, *A six weeks' tour in the Highlands of Scotland*, London, 1851.

Grantown... is a dull uniform village, not quite so uniform as Rothes, but duller. A man who had amassed some hundreds as sergeant and messman in the army has taken a small inn here, the Grants Arms. His wife, a forward, vulgar, handsomish woman, from Portsmouth, seems to hold Grantown in great contempt... These foolish people have wasted their money in plate, in an expensive mahogany sideboard, good mahogany chairs, with hair bottoms and brass nails, and most expensive bed-steads, the house not being better than a village alehouse, and out of the way or possibility of much custom.

SOUTHEY, R, *Journal of a tour in Scotland in* 1819, London, 1929.

# Gretna Green, Dumfriesshire

Instead of the healthy peasant, and the neat cottage, which adorn the most remote English villages, my eyes encountered, in a cluster of mud build sheds, a number of miserable wretches, ragged, bare footed, and squalid, almost beyond the power of description... Such wretchedness is naturally the offspring of idleness, ignorance, and necessity.

SKRINE, H, *Tours in the north of England and great part of Scotland*, London, 1795.

At Gretna Green, we had the curiosity to call upon the high priest of Hymen. It was at an early hour in the morning, and we could not be favoured with his society, without paying its price in whisky. A quart of this fiery spirit he drank before his breakfast.

MAWMAN, J, *An Excursion to the Highlands of Scotland and the English Lakes*, London, 1805.

The peasantry are cast in a rougher mould – their faces are thinner, cheek bones higher, and the expression of countenance far more reflective. On the other hand it must be allowed that the females are far less pleasing in person, than the fairer and ruddier daughters of the south.

MCLELLAN, H, *Journal of a Residence in Scotland*, Boston, 1834.

It is a dreary place; the stone houses dirty and miserable, with broken windows.

WORDSWORTH, D, *Recollections of a tour made in Scotland A.D. 1803*. Edinburgh, 1875.

# Gruinard Bay, Ross and Cromarty

There is nothing at Loch Gruinard, nor in the surrounding country, which can induce an ordinary traveller to bestow his time on it.

MacCULLOCH, J *The Highlands and Western Isles of Scotland*, London, 1824.

# Haddington, East Lothian

Haddington, at present most wretched in its appearance, was once tolerably prosperous.

MAWMAN, J, *An Excursion to the Highlands of Scotland and the English Lakes*, London, 1805.

# Halkirk, Caithness

The time was, and not many years ago, when your Caithness ghillie would tramp continually over moor and moss laden with grouse for one shilling a day. Now, however, everything appertaining to sporting is so much more expensive than formerly, that a ghillie will ask three shillings a day, and not work less for half a crown, expecting besides his breakfast and luncheon, and an unlimited quantity of whisky.

WELD, C, *Two months in the Highlands, Orcadia, and Skye*, London, 1860.

We had a piper, who, though he had not had the advantage of being taught at the great bagpipe college in Skye... nevertheless played extremely well. To be sure, it was sometimes necessary to station him in a distant room, as the skirl was a little too harsh to be enjoyed at close quarters, particularly when John Gunn made too free with the whisky, without which, however, it was not easy to get John to play at all.

WELD, C, *Two months in the Highlands, Orcadia, and Skye*, London, 1860.

# Hamilton, Lanarkshire

The disgusting custom of the native women walking bare feet
was on this occasion particularly striking.

SHAW, S, *A Tour, in 1787, from London to the Western Highlands of
Scotland*, London, 1788.

We entered Hamilton, and applied at the first public house
which we saw, for some dinner, but a very stout fellow
answered in a surly tone, that he had none for us... We asked
at the next house with a sign, and an old wretch, a very hag...
with matted locks and squalid face, and diabolical expression of
countenance, yelled out, that we should get about our business
directly, for she would let us have nothing... We tried a third
abode... and were stopped ere we crossed the threshold, and
denied admittance by both host and hostess, a couple of young
and dirty people... We now staggered into the Buck's-head
Inn... Here... on a very filthy table cloth, we procured some
tolerably good cold mutton, vile dough half baked mutton pies,
stuff which was called pastry, and cheese so dirty that we had
not time and leisure to ascertain its colour.

BRISTED, J, *A Pedestrian Tour through part of the Highlands of Scotland in
1801*, London, 1803.

A considerable but dirty town.

CARR, J, *Caledonian Sketches or A Tour through Scotland in 1807*,
London, 1809.

A small town of no great note.

LONDONER, *North of England and Scotland in 1704*, Edinburgh, 1818.

There was nothing remarkable in the treatment we met
with at this inn, except the lazy impertinence of the waiter...
The house thoroughly dirty.

WORDSWORTH, D, *Recollections of a tour made in Scotland
A.D.* 1803. Edinburgh, 1875.

Hamilton is a dirty old town, with a good many thatched
houses in the street - implying either poverty, or great
disregard of danger from fire.

SOUTHEY, R, *Journal of a tour in Scotland in* 1819, London, 1929.

## Hamilton Palace

Its situation is by no means eligible, either in point of
convenience or beauty.

CARTER, N, *Letters from Europe comprising The Journal of a Tour through...
Scotland... in* 1825, New York, 1827.

# Hawick, Roxburghshire
## Inn

The inn looked large, but the inside of it was very dirty and
uncomfortable... There is but one sitting room at Hawick; and
only one tolerable bed chamber, with two beds in it... The town
of Hawick is old and shabby... I left the uncomfortable inn
with pleasure very early.

MURRAY, S, *A Companion and Useful Guide to the Beauties of Scotland*,
London, 1799.

# The Highlands

It was, till very lately, a practice throughout the Highlands, to blood their cattle now and then for the sake of their blood; which, having boiled with a little oatmeal, they eat. This, though little short of Abyssinian savageness, is certain beyond all doubt; nor is the practice in some parts of the Hebrides, Caithness, and Ross-shire, to this day wholly laid aside.

HALL, J, *Travels in Scotland by an unusual route*, London, 1807.

I am very reluctantly compelled, by a regard to truth, to bear witness to the fact noticed by Dr. Samuel Johnson, that the lower sort of the Highlanders are greatly addicted to lying; as well as they formerly were to stealing... The most general impression that remained on my mind was the marked difference between what I had seen of the Highlanders and Lowlanders. The Lowlanders are certainly far before the Highlanders in civilisation and all the arts, and much more industrious. They are also... more cheerful and lively than the Highlanders. The Highlanders are fond of dancing, when roused by the bagpipe or other music, but they are at bottom gloomy and melancholy... They have not any very accurate notions of the natural turpitude of either lying or stealing, though they are afraid of the gallows. In the interior parts, there are yet striking remains of savage manners.

HALL, J, *Travels in Scotland by an unusual route*, London, 1807.

The great faults of the common people in the Highlands
are laziness and an inordinate attachment to whisky, a
strong spirituous liquor. So lazy are many of them, that
they rather choose to lounge about idle, and half starved,
than work and be well fed. Yet, rouse their attention, and
show them any prospect that promises success, and they
become active, enterprising and persevering; in this respect
resembling the Cherokee Indians, and most other nations
only verging towards improvement.

HALL, J, *Travels in Scotland by an unusual route*, London, 1807.

The gentry may be said to be a handsome people,
but the commonalty much otherwise; one would
hardly think, by their faces, they were of the same
species, at least of the same country, which plainly
proceeds from their bad food, smoke at home, and sun,
wind, and rain abroad.

BURT, E & JAMIESON, R, *Letters from a Gentleman in the North of
Scotland to his friend in London*, London, 1818.

The common habit of the ordinary Highlanders is far from
being acceptable to the eye. This dress is called the kilt; and,
for the most part, they wear the petticoat so very short, that
in a windy day, going up a hill, or stooping, the indecency
of it is plainly discovered... The plaid serves the ordinary
people for a cloak by day and the bedding at night; by the
latter it imbibes so much perspiration, that no one day can
free it from the filthy smell; and even some of better than
ordinary appearance, when the plaid falls from the shoulder...

toss it over again... which conveys the offence in whiffs that are intolerable.

BURT, E & JAMIESON, R, *Letters from a Gentleman in the North of Scotland to his friend in London*, London, 1818.

The young children of the ordinary Highlanders are miserable objects indeed, and are mostly over-run with that distemper which some of the old men are hardly ever freed of from their infancy. I have often seen them come out from the huts early in a cold morning stark naked, and squat themselves down (if I might decently use the comparison) like dogs on a dunghill.

BURT, E & JAMIESON, R, *Letters from a Gentleman in the North of Scotland to his friend in London*, London, 1818.

The lower class of Highlanders are generally ugly.

DE SAUSSURE, L, *A Voyage to the Hebrides*, London, 1822.

The Highland Laird partakes much more of the Irish character than I had ever been taught to suppose. He has the same profusion, the same recklessness, the same rapacity; but he has more power, and he uses it worse... A few of these are desirous of improving their own estates by bettering the condition of the tenants. But the greater number are fools at heart, with neither understanding nor virtue, nor good nature to form such a wish. Their object is to increase their revenue, and they care not by what means this is accomplished.

SOUTHEY, R, *Journal of a tour in Scotland in* 1819, London, 1929.

SCOTLAND THE WORST

# Hoy, Orkney

At a little township we called for the most active rock man
or bird hunter of the island, and engaged him to go lyre
{shearwater} catching the next morning... The young are very
fat, and much relished by the natives.

NEILL, P, *A Tour through some of the islands of Orkney and Shetland*,
Edinburgh, 1806.

# Huna, John o' Groats, Caithness
## Inn

We found Huna not a village... but a scattered hamlet; one of
the meanest cottages of which claims the designation of an inn.
In addition to the discomforts of indifferent accommodation
and poor fare, the only apartment appropriated to travellers
was occupied by a group of drunken unruly fellows
from Stroma – smugglers by profession – who had been
plundered by a revenue officer and compelled to carry
their contraband commodity to his very door. The more
copious their libations... the more obstreperous became their
language and bearing.

SUTHERLAND, A, *A Summer Ramble in the North Highlands*,
Edinburgh, 1825.

# Huntly, Aberdeenshire

I came to Strathbogie, a small pitiful village, but a very
proper name, it being on every side boggy
and marshy ground.

VOLUNTEER, *A Journey through part of England and Scotland...
in the year* 1746, London, 1747.

# Inchture, Perthshire

We... made our way... into a place baptized a parlour,
where every sense was more than disgusted; sight, smell,
feeling, &c. &c. were assailed by such a combination of
beastly and abominable objects, that we could scarcely
endure existence. The hearth was composed of clay,
kneaded into the form of a trough, which was nearly full
of stale urine; the table was ornamented, in broad patches,
with horse dung, ale-spillings, egg-leavings, remains of
cascading, and other filth... In short I never witnessed any
scene so entirely filthy, horrible, and sickening as was this
parlour, where we were to breakfast.

BRISTED, J, *A Pedestrian Tour through part of the Highlands of Scotland in*
1801, London, 1803.

# Inverarnan, Perthshire
## Inn

We came to a dreary vagabond inn without any sign, where
we were nearly poisoned by heath smoke and other filth...

At length, she got for us something which she called hung mutton... One mouthful of this delicious fare so effectually satisfied us, that I know not if actual starvation could have induced us to venture on a second.

BRISTED, J, *A Pedestrian Tour through part of the Highlands of Scotland in 1801*, London, 1803.

Arrived at Glen Falloch; inn very bad.

THORNTON, T, *A Sporting Tour through the Northern parts of England and great part of the Highlands of Scotland*. London, 1804.

Weak as lambs, we went to be flea-bitten at Inverarnan Inn. Oh! but it is a dirty place, and I would rather lie down among the heather, or trudge on ten long miles, then sleep - or rather watch - there again.

TOWNSHEND, C, *A Descriptive Tour of Scotland*, London, 1840.

# Inveraray, Argyllshire

As for the town of Inveraray, it is hardly worth notice, being a small, inconsiderable fishing place.

THORNTON, T, *A Sporting Tour through the Northern parts of England and great part of the Highlands of Scotland*. London, 1804.

One of those travelling collectors, called English Riders, came... to Inveraray. He stayed day after day, delaying his departure, until there should be some appearance of fair weather. At last, his patience being exhausted, he swore hastily to the landlord, that he believed it rained every day... at Inveraray. 'Hoot, no,' replied the landlord, 'it snows sometimes.'

HALL, J, *Travels in Scotland by an unusual route*, London, 1807.

The town itself is rather miserable.

TOWNSHEND, C, *A Descriptive Tour of Scotland*, London, 1840.

At the beginning of this our second walk we passed through the town, which is but a doleful example of Scotch filth.

WORDSWORTH, D, *Recollections of a tour made in Scotland A.D.* 1803. Edinburgh, 1875.

## Inveraray Castle

Inveraray Castle... not a very tasteful building.

TOWNSHEND, C, *A Descriptive Tour of Scotland*, London, 1840.

The castle is abominable... In its ordinary state, Inveraray to me is a scene of heavy dullness.

COCKBURN, H, *Circuit Journeys by the late Lord Cockburn*, Edinburgh, 1889.

# Inverbervie, Kincardineshire

A miserable small place.

VOLUNTEER, *A Journey through part of England and Scotland... in the year 1746*, London, 1747.

The town, externally looks filthy and insignificant: internally it is mean, ill-built, and devoid of everything worth of notice.

Great numbers of squalid children and filthy ducks waddle about the street.

SUTHERLAND, A, *A Summer Ramble in the North Highlands*, Edinburgh, 1825.

Bervie is an ugly town; larger, but not much better than the assemblage of poor houses at the harbour.

SOUTHEY, R, *Journal of a tour in Scotland in* 1819, London, 1929.

# Invergordon, Ross and Cromarty

Invergordon where we breakfasted is an ugly village.

SOUTHEY, R, *Journal of a tour in Scotland in* 1819, London, 1929.

# Invermoriston, Inverness-shire

## Inn

We arrived next morning before breakfast at Invermoriston, where a change of administration was taking place at the inn... Nothing is done in the Highlands without an accompaniment of whisky, the flavour of which pervaded every corner of the house so powerfully, that any tee-totaller would have committed a breach of his oath, by merely inhaling the air, while the waiter had no time to wait, the maid was as useless and sulky as an American help, and the horses were all absent on perpetual leave.

SINCLAIR, C, *Scotland and the Scotch*, New York, 1840.

The one at Invermoriston ought to be good... As it is, it is shameful. But it is not a bad specimen of what is called a good

Scotch country inn, because, though they knew of our coming, and had seen it pouring all day, they had neither fire nor food prepared, a tea tray was receiving the rain from the skylight of what was given me to dress in; and the landlord, though married only last week, was drunk.

COCKBURN, H, *Circuit Journeys by the late Lord Cockburn*, Edinburgh, 1889.

# Inverness, Inverness-shire

A small dirty poor place.

VOLUNTEER, *A Journey through part of England and Scotland... in the year 1746*, London, 1747.

To the sides of this river, the washer women come to wash their linen... by treading it in a tub with their naked feet, and holding at the same time their petticoats up to their middle... you'll see in a warm morning, the river edges lined with these sort of women that are maid servants, and frequently as many soldiers admiring their legs and thighs.

VOLUNTEER, *A Journey through part of England and Scotland... in the year 1746*, London, 1747.

This town above all others in Scotland, is noted for handsome women, and indeed there's many agreeable girls, with whom it requires very little trouble to get acquainted with.

VOLUNTEER, *A Journey through part of England and Scotland... in the year 1746*, London, 1747.

Streets narrow and dirty.

THOMSON, W, *Tour in England and Scotland in 1785*, London, 1788.

Your servant must be careful of what water he gives his horses
at Inverness, or they will get ill.

MURRAY, S, *A Companion and Useful Guide to the Beauties of Scotland*,
London, 1799.

Some of the houses in it are tolerably built, but the streets are
narrow and dirty.

THORNTON, T, *A Sporting Tour through the Northern parts
of England and great part of the Highlands of Scotland.*
London, 1804.

Some of the inns in these remote parts... are not very inviting;
your chamber, to which you sometimes enter from without
doors, by stairs as dirty as the streets... But it is nauseous
to see the walls and inside of the curtains spotted, as if
everyone that had lain there had spit straight forward in
whatever position they lay.

BURT, E & JAMIESON, R, *Letters from a Gentleman in the North of
Scotland to his friend in London*, London, 1818.

As to a description of the coffee room... I shall venture to tell
you in general, that the room appears as if it had never been
cleaned since the building of the house.

BURT, E & JAMIESON, R, *Letters from a Gentleman in the North of
Scotland to his friend in London*, London, 1818.

The chasms in the inside and middle of these walls, and the
disproportionate quantity of mortar, by comparison, with
the stone, render them receptacles for prodigious numbers
of rats... where they burrow and breed securely, and by

that means abound everywhere in the small Scots towns, especially near the sea.

BURT, E & JAMIESON, R, *Letters from a Gentleman in the North of Scotland to his friend in London*, London, 1818.

The extreme parts of town are made up of most miserably low, dirty hovels, faced and covered with turf, with a bottomless tub, or basket, in the roof for a chimney.

BURT, E & JAMIESON, R, *Letters from a Gentleman in the North of Scotland to his friend in London*, London, 1818.

In this little town there are no less than four natural fools. The beggars are numerous, and exceedingly importunate, for there is no parish allowance to any.

BURT, E & JAMIESON, R, *Letters from a Gentleman in the North of Scotland to his friend in London*, London, 1818.

One of the most remarkable qualities of the Ness water is its tendency to affect strangers who drink it with temporary diarrhoea.

ANDERSON, G & ANDERSON, P, *Guide to the Highlands and Islands of Scotland*, London, 1834.

The lower orders... are almost all coarse and uncomely, mostly yellow skinned, with large freckles. Inverness has been injured in its beauty... by the erection, on a very conspicuous position, of a very ugly Free Kirk school.

COCKBURN, H, *Circuit Journeys by the late Lord Cockburn*, Edinburgh, 1889.

The canal here was under the superintendence of Mr Davidson, a strange, cynical humorist... He used to say, of

Inverness, that if justice were done to the inhabitants there would be nobody left there in the course of twenty years but the Provost and the Hangman.

SOUTHEY, R, *Journal of a tour in Scotland in 1819*, London, 1929.

# Inversnaid, Stirlingshire
## Inversnaid Inn

We had a wait of about two hours at this place until the steamer arrived, during which the different tourists... were engaged in seeking what refreshments were to be had; but these proved very scanty, the staple articles being whisky and a watery fluid, which the guide wife dignified with the name and price of Edinburgh ale.

PEDESTRIAN, *A six weeks' tour in the Highlands of Scotland*, London, 1851.

Perhaps this invocation of a blessing on steam was not quite unconnected with the contrast between the luxurious table d'hôte of the steamer, and the sordid accommodation, which we found in the Inversnaid Locanda.

JOHNSON, J, *The Recess or Autumnal relaxations in the Highlands and Lowlands*, London, 1834.

The country people... are an ugly race, but the expression of their countenances is usually good.

TOWNSHEND, C, *A Descriptive Tour of Scotland*, London, 1840.

# Irvine, Ayrshire

Abounds not in good inns.

HERON, R, *Observations made in a journey through the Western Counties of Scotland in the autumn of* 1792, Perth, 1793.

# Islay, Argyllshire

Though Islay is considerably different from Jura, it is not very interesting to a traveller.

MacCULLOCH, J *The Highlands and Western Isles of Scotland*, London, 1824.

# Isle of Barra, Outer Hebrides

As the inhabitants of Barra seem to have less intercourse with the mainland, or continent, as they term it, then either the inhabitants of the Orkney, Shetland, or the other Hebrides, so they are evidently less polished, and more shy and stupid.

HALL, J, *Travels in Scotland by an unusual route*, London, 1807.

It is a draw back on the merits of the Barra men, that they are addicted to the use of whisky; a propensity fostered by their great gains as much as by their mode of life. The ancient prowess of the Highlanders in this respect, is well known; and, like their ancestors, the Scythians, they were notorious for quarrelling over their cups.

MacCULLOCH, J *The Highlands and Western Isles of Scotland*, London, 1824.

Most of the hovels abound in uncomfortable parasites, and are contiguous to stagnant pools, tainted with animal refuse, around, in, and about which the half naked and half starved children play.

GRAY, T, *Barra, in the Outer Hebrides*, Nature and Art, Vol. 1, London, 1866.

A robust woman, broad in the shoulders, thick necked, large handed, bare legged, her hair half way down her back, and a short, ragged garment, with little or no covering for her head, is of the ordinary type in Barra.

GRAY, T, *Barra, in the Outer Hebrides*, Nature and Art, Vol. 1, London, 1866.

Every man's hand is, so to speak, against his neighbour. As a practical fact we found that almost everyone had something to tell confidentially about someone else that would have insured hanging or transportation for life if true and proved.

GRAY, T, *Barra, in the Outer Hebrides*, Nature and Art, Vol. 1, London, 1866.

At the cleanest and best {inn} we had to sleep on a table, in a place with a brick floor and ducks for visitors... Let its name be recorded as Sinclair's Inn, Borve, Barra.

GRAY, T, *Barra, in the Outer Hebrides*, Nature and Art, Vol. 1, London, 1866.

The police force in the island is not active and is not
intelligent, not could it establish a character for sobriety.
It consists of a solitary constable.

GRAY, T, *Barra, in the Outer Hebrides*, Nature and Art, Vol. 1,
London, 1866.

# Isle of Bute, County of Bute

We could not catch a cicerone anywhere... till at last a boy
of fourteen appeared, smoking his pipe; and he seemed
to have smoked away any brains he ever had, being
most incomparably stupid.

SINCLAIR, C, *Scotland and the Scotch*, New York, 1840.

## Kean's Cottage

Kean sacrificed the picturesque for good solid brick and mortar
comfort, not even indulging our eyes with a thatched roof, but
substituting a steep, ugly, substantial canopy of slates... while
the large, square, matter of fact windows, gave a last finish
to its ugliness.

SINCLAIR, C, *Scotland and the Scotch*, New York, 1840.

# Isle of Iona, Argyllshire

Even before we touched land, we were besieged by a troop
of half naked amphibious looking boys who emulously

presented to our notice plates full of Iona pebbles, and, as we walked on towards the ruins, other tribes kept persecuting us and poking their plates in our faces, ever crying out... 'gie us a bawbie!' At length the nuisance became so intolerable that we were forced to turn and face the enemy and, charging them with our sticks, compel them to retire to a respectful distance.

TOWNSHEND, C, *A Descriptive Tour of Scotland*, London, 1840.

# Isle of Jura, Argyllshire

Intimate as I am with Jura, I have little to say of it, and much less to say in its favour.

MacCULLOCH, J *The Highlands and Western Isles of Scotland*, London, 1824.

# Isle of Lewis, Outer Hebrides

Although destitution, immorality, and degradation abound there, as they do everywhere in the Outer Hebrides, the people are better off in Lewis than in any of the other islands of the group, excepting perhaps, North Uist.

GRAY, T, *Barra, in the Outer Hebrides*, Nature and Art, Vol. 1, London, 1866.

# Isle of Mull, Argyllshire

The appearance of Mull itself is singularly dreary and barren.

JOHNSON, J, *The Recess or Autumnal relaxations in the Highlands and Lowlands*, London, 1834.

# Isle of Skye, Inverness-shire

The clothing of the female population of Skye is hence generally coarse and mean in the extreme... The old women throw a dirty blanket over their shoulders... An air of squalid penury, too, soon settles about them; and in middle age their prematurely pinched, care and penury worn features, are far from engaging.

ANDERSON, G & ANDERSON, P, *Guide to the Highlands and Islands of Scotland*, London, 1834.

The Skye cottages cannot be said to enliven and embellish the scenery, as they are the most mournful looking dwellings I ever beheld.

SINCLAIR, C, *Scotland and the Scotch*, New York, 1840.

My walk to Dunvegan (eight miles) was far from pleasant, being chiefly remembered by the meteorological varieties of rain, mist, and wind... But if you go to Skye, you must expect more rain than sunshine; and you will do well to remember as you trudge along that the peasants you see are permanent dwellers amidst this bleakness and poverty.

WELD, C, *Two months in the Highlands, Orcadia, and Skye*, London, 1860.

Their hearts delight is to take plenty of time over their work. They are quite ready to plod away to any extent, and are hard working and hard living – but oh! how slow... The Saxon is considered fair game, and may be fleeced to the utmost possible limit; whereas a fellow Highlander is rarely overcharged, except along the regular tourists routes, where the 'morale' of the people is always rapidly destroyed, and even the children are taught by travellers to run beside the coaches and beg.
GORDON-CUMMING, C, *From the Hebrides to the Himalayas*, London, 1876.

Small flies, alias midges... the little miscreants are the very torture of life in Skye. They start in ravenous armed myriads, making work utterly impossible, till at last, with fevered blood, and face and hands literally swollen by their attacks... you have to leave the spot.
GORDON-CUMMING, C, *From the Hebrides to the Himalayas*, London, 1876.

## Broadford

At Broadford there is a picturesque dish of milk set on the table at four o'clock, with salt, mustard, and knives and forks. The problem is how to eat milk with a knife and fork.
MacCULLOCH, J *The Highlands and Western Isles of Scotland*, London, 1824.

This very poor dull inn... We got the best room in the house: but bad is the best. At this moment I am writing in our double bedded desolate chamber, whose bare walls have once been whitewashed: but now great spots of damp appear through

the cracked and peeling plaster; the beds are furnished with
the commonest red checked cotton hangings not over clean;
the uncarpeted floor.

TOWNSHEND, C, *A Descriptive Tour of Scotland*, London, 1840.

I thought Broadford had been a town... a real town or respectable
village. But I find that it consists of three houses, the inn, the
school, and 'the shop' near which there are a dozen or two of
hovels... till we came up to the holes which are termed the doors,
and saw the ragged human rabbits looking out of the warren, we
did not take them to be houses... The badness of this inn, is only
not just as bad as Shiel House.

COCKBURN, H, *Circuit Journeys by the late Lord Cockburn*,
Edinburgh, 1889.

## Ardvasar Inn

It was a hovel of one storey, with earthen floor, where, perhaps,
in times of pampered nicety, I might have hesitated to set foot...
The little jolly inn is certainly 'the most villainous house in all
Scotland for fleas.'

TOWNSHEND, C, *A Descriptive Tour of Scotland*, London, 1840.

## Sligachan Inn

With the exception of those at Portree and Broadford, all
the other inns in Skye are sorry taverns, where you must be
prepared to rough it in bed and board... Sligachan Inn at no
period of the year can be a lively abode... you may suppose
that its few eligibilities are very much at a discount... The

house itself was extremely uncomfortable... It was very easy to see that the domesticities of Sligachan were out of joint, for the landlady neglected her duty, and the landlord went about the house with a heavy heart. And no wonder, for when you hear that his wife was not allowed access to the liquor closet, you will understand that she was not fit for the office of landlady. Occasionally I found occupation in re-lighting the fire, which had been suddenly extinguished by a waterfall down the chimney.

WELD, C, *Two months in the Highlands, Orcadia, and Skye*, London, 1860.

## Uig Inn

The appearance of this inn was far from prepossessing, and when I looked more closely into the domesticities, I was almost led to abandon my intention of sleeping here... When I woke in the morning I had reason to be thankful that I was proof against the attacks of at least one species of nocturnal animal; for I saw three make a slow retreat beneath the bolster.

WELD, C, *Two months in the Highlands, Orcadia, and Skye*, London, 1860.

## Loch Coruisk

Not a wreath of friendly mist was there to lend mystery to the scene, but far up the valley a party of odious tourists were making the sad hills echo their vulgar shouts.

GORDON-CUMMING, C, *From the Hebrides to the Himalayas*, London, 1876.

# Quiraing

As a general rule, tourists visiting the Quiraing only come by the coach, and 'do' the rocks in a couple of hours, during which a fair amount of whisky is consumed, and the echoes are awakened by discordant shouts and songs... The excellent roads make this easy enough; and at the time of our visit, rival coaches had reduced one another's prices to such a pitch, that they were carrying passengers at one penny per mile.

GORDON-CUMMING, C, *From the Hebrides to the Himalayas*, London, 1876.

# Jedburgh, Roxburghshire

Melrose and its associates were most beautiful. But on the whole I think Jedburgh the better place of the two; not perhaps in its actual and present state, for it is squalid in daily increasing poverty, but in its possibilities.

COCKBURN, H, *Circuit Journeys by the late Lord Cockburn*, Edinburgh, 1889.

# Kelso, Roxburghshire

Great regulations might be made about dancing, which would tend to make the assembly more acceptable to strangers: indeed, throughout Scotland, there is a strange custom, which is disgusting to an Englishman. Though a lady is engaged as a partner for the evening, she conceives herself entitled to jump up and dance a reel with any indifferent person, without saying a syllable to her partner. Many disagreeable situations I have seen gentlemen thrown into, from not knowing this custom, which, though established, I cannot think well bred.

THORNTON, T, *A Sporting Tour through the Northern parts of England and great part of the Highlands of Scotland*. London, 1804.

I asked her what was to be had, and she told me potted pigeons... The cloth was laid, but I was too unwilling to grease my fingers to touch it; and presently after, the pot of pigeons was set on the table. When I came to examine my delicacy, there were two or three of the pigeons lay mangled in the pot, and behind were the furrows, in the butter, of those fingers that had raked them out of it and the butter itself needed no close application to discover its quality. My disgust at this sight was so great... and although the night was approaching, I called for my horses, and marched off... and met with yet worse entertainment at a little house which was my next quarters... Here I was told I might have a breast of mutton... but when it was brought me, it appeared to have been smoked and dried in the chimney corner; and it looked like the glue that hangs up in an ironmonger's shop: this, you may believe, was very disgusting to the eye... When I had been conducted to my lodging room, I found the curtains of my bed were very foul by being handled by the dirty wenches.

BURT, E & JAMIESON, R, *Letters from a Gentleman in the North of Scotland to his friend in London*, London, 1818.

# Kenmore, Perthshire

We now, by a rapid descent, reached the village, of which the inn seems to be the principal house... we have obtained a capital breakfast, ministered to us by as capital a waiter, whose jolly nose, much resembling a bunch of red grapes, seemed to promise comfortable things.

TOWNSHEND, C, *A Descriptive Tour of Scotland*, London, 1840.

# Isle of Kerrera, Argyllshire

Passing onwards, we gave a disapproving look at the island of Kerrera, where we saw nothing to admire.

SINCLAIR, C, *Scotland and the Scotch*, New York, 1840.

# Kilbarchan, Renfrewshire

A still more considerable class are the keepers of tippling houses: and these seem to be the most thriving in the village. In the morning, at mid-day, in the evening – whenever there is a penny in the purse, these people eagerly repair to the dram shop.

HERON, R, *Observations made in a journey through the Western Counties of Scotland in the autumn of* 1792, Perth, 1793.

# Kilchrenan, Argyllshire

A small but wretched looking village... The sacrament was
being celebrated... In the church yard... the minister appeared
solemnly engaged in prayer; whilst at the public house, not a
hundred yards distant from the kirk, numbers were engaged
in drinking, with great noise and merriment, every room,
every corner was full, and crowds were taking their drams at
the door; men and women, young and old, alike joined in this
revelry... The scene was disgusting... The truly religious come
to enjoy the sacred ordinance; whilst the idle and profane
come to meet their companions, and to seek pleasure in
dissipation and vice.

PEDESTRIAN, *A six weeks' tour in the Highlands of Scotland,*
London, 1851.

# Killicrankie, Perthshire

In the far famed Pass of Killicrankie, I confess
I was much disappointed.

JOHNSON, J, *The Recess or Autumnal relaxations in the Highlands and
Lowlands,* London, 1834.

# Killin, Perthshire

## Killin Inn

At Killin is a very bad inn, very dear, and very dirty, bad wine,
bad bread; in short, if you have nothing of your own with you

to eat and drink, you will be very ill off; besides, the landlord in 1796, was a drunken saucy creature; and charged much higher, and provided far worse entertainment, both for man and beast, than any other innkeeper I met with. The misfortune is, there is but one inn at Killin, and there you must sleep.

MURRAY, S, *A Companion and Useful Guide to the Beauties of Scotland*, London, 1799.

The Killin innkeeper exhibited a remarkable illustration of the inner and stronger fortification by which a Scotchman is surrounded - the love of self. The interest of his neighbour in Kenmore could not be thought of, while there was any chance of furthering his own.

JOHNSON, J, *The Recess or Autumnal relaxations in the Highlands and Lowlands*, London, 1834.

I fancy that all the people about Killin partake of the sleepy, melancholy character of its low situation... Matters were not much mended when I lay down in my cupboard at the inn. The little crib, in which I was penned for the night, reminded me extremely of the corpse bins of the Breadalbane cemetery.

TOWNSHEND, C, *A Descriptive Tour of Scotland*, London, 1840.

# Killin/Tyndrum

At about eight miles from Killin towards Tyndrum, there are two public houses, near to each other; equally bad... At neither of these houses, can you, or your servant, eat anything they can give you with comfort; and it is impossible to sleep there, both houses being mere dirty huts.

MURRAY, S, *A Companion and Useful Guide to the Beauties of Scotland*, London, 1799.


# Killin/Kenmore

We then crawled into the most filthy room, without exception, that we had ever seen, and were presented with a very small basin of very sour milk, not good butter, and that deplorable bannock, which had already nearly terminated my existence by inducing a desperate diarrhoea, that weakened me to the very verge of evanescence.

BRISTED, J, *A Pedestrian Tour through part of the Highlands of Scotland in 1801*, London, 1803.

We... were waited on by a lad in a Highland kilt which was not too long in its dimensions. We began to discourse... upon the Highlanders, occasioned by our waiter's short kilt flapping about rather unseemly whenever he exerted himself briskly, for the improvement and edification of the females... Why is the kilt which seems to be a dress more than bordering on indecency, still continued... Partly from convenience, because it allows full play to the lower extremities, and facilitates the bounding of the honest Highlander over his native hills.

BRISTED, J, *A Pedestrian Tour through part of the Highlands of Scotland in 1801*, London, 1803.

## Suie Inn, near Killin

We had a bad supper, and the next morning they made us an unreasonable charge; and the servant was uncivil, because forsooth! we had no wine.

WORDSWORTH, D, *Recollections of a tour made in Scotland A.D.* 1803. Edinburgh, 1875.

# Kilmarnock, Ayrshire

The natives in this northern latitude are naturally so addicted to idleness and nastiness, that should not the heavens contribute the blessings of rain, they would inevitably surfeit with their own cleanliness.

FRANCK, R, *Northern Memoirs calculated for the Meridian of Scotland... writ in the year* 1658, Edinburgh, 1821.

# Kinghorn, Fife

A straggling dirty town, chiefly inhabited by fishermen, and hirers (people that keep horses for let) for these Kinghorn hirers are known all over Scotland, for their impudence and impositions.

VOLUNTEER, *A Journey through part of England and Scotland... in the year* 1746, London, 1747.

# Kingussie, Inverness-shire

Day charming; went to church... It appeared to me that the men came here to eat tobacco, and the women to sleep. I may venture to affirm, that a tax on sleeping females at church would bring in, from this parish, a pretty revenue.

THORNTON, T, *A Sporting Tour through the Northern parts of England and great part of the Highlands of Scotland*. London, 1804.

Can scarcely be described as a flourishing village.

ANDERSON, G & ANDERSON, P, *Guide to the Highlands and Islands of Scotland*, London, 1834.

We are now in the Gordon Arms Hotel at Kingussie, with the loudest bells and strongest teethed rats I have ever encountered.

COCKBURN, H, *Circuit Journeys by the late Lord Cockburn*, Edinburgh, 1889.

## Old Pitmain Inn

An abominable hostel, but it had served the public, I suppose, at least one hundred years, and all this time had received that sort of welcome which is given by a vessel in distress to the only port it has to repair to.

COCKBURN, H, *Circuit Journeys by the late Lord Cockburn*, Edinburgh, 1889.

# Kinlochewe, Ross and Cromarty

The very poor public house.

*The Highlands of Scotland*, Issue 326, The Penny Magazine,
London, 1837.

# Kinloch Rannoch, Perthshire

For indeed the gastronomy of this country is not commendable:
nor aught that is connected with it... At this very Kinloch
Rannoch, you are promised kale, good mutton kale... and find
a species of barley water, spangled with the glittering drops
elicited from a few mutton bones, in which it is difficult to
discover whether the meat or the bone is hardest... Whatever
you do, beware of that thing called a mutton chop. Boiled fowls
you may know by the impossibility of eating them... and roasted
ones, by the blackness of their skins.

MacCULLOCH, J *The Highlands and Western Isles of Scotland*,
London, 1824.

# Kinross, Kinross-shire

Donaldson's, at the north end of the town, is rather the
best inn; neither of them extremely good.

MURRAY, S, *A Companion and Useful Guide to the Beauties of Scotland*,
London, 1799.

The town of Kinross, which, sooth to say, is somewhat mean and dirty, is scattered along the banks of Loch Leven... Compared with the rich scenes we had so lately quitted, the whole country about Kinross has a desolate and poverty stricken appearance; but, after we had left the town and proceeded for some distance along the road to Alloa, the scenery improved in cheerfulness and beauty.

TOWNSHEND, C, *A Descriptive Tour of Scotland,* London, 1840.

The principal street being in the line of the great North Road, is enlivened by continual passage, but the other parts of the town are mean and wretched.

PEDESTRIAN, *A six weeks' tour in the Highlands of Scotland,* London, 1851.

# Kintyre, Argyllshire

As for the bannocks, they are deal boards made easy, and taste like a compressed mixture of bran and chaff. They hurt the teeth, and cause a sensation in the throat... As for the milk, it is not every southerner past the age of infancy, who is possessed of sufficient bodily and stomachic power to drink a glass of it before dinner without materially interfering with his digestion for the remainder of the day.

BEDE, C, *Glencreggan or, A Highland home in Cantyre,* London, 1861.

Approaching a farmhouse in Kintyre...you must pick your way carefully; for although liquid manure may be a very useful thing in its proper place, yet it is not precisely that odorous compound in which we should prefer to bathe the boots that will afterwards bear us into the presence of ladies... we presently pass to deposits of filth through which we must boldly pass with bated breath, though not averted eye... Here comes Mr Mac's milkmaid, setting us the example how we ought to walk, by paddling through all the dirty messes with her still dirtier feet. They are naked of course, and are visible to some distance above the ankle; and very unpleasant in the prospect.

BEDE, C, *Glencreggan or, A Highland home in Cantyre*, London, 1861.

I must say, that the Highland lassie, however picturesque an object, would be made a much more wholesome and inviting character by a little more attention to tidiness and cleanliness.

BEDE, C, *Glencreggan or, A Highland home in Cantyre*, London, 1861.

# Kirkcaldy, Fife

At a little, not very dirty, public house, I am now writing my diary, with some gin, water, and not swallowable biscuits... Indeed, such tough, unbiteable matter as the biscuits, we had never before seen, handled, or met with.

BRISTED, J, *A Pedestrian Tour through part of the Highlands of Scotland in 1801*, London, 1803.

# Kirk of Shotts, Lanarkshire

Stopped at the Kirk of Shotts, but found the inn so bad, and the whole house so inebriated, that we did not take off the horses.

THORNTON, T, *A Sporting Tour through the Northern parts of England and great part of the Highlands of Scotland*. London, 1804.


# Kirkpatrick, Dumfriesshire

I would not have the numbers of the people increased, their industry quickened, or their enjoyments multiplied, at the expense of their virtues... Crowded together, and continually supplied with money, the workmen, in those towns, hold an almost perpetual holiday... They become, by consequence extravagant, debauched, idle and knavish... Races, cock fighting, and festive meetings for the purpose solely of festivity, ought to be carefully discouraged.

HERON, R, *Observations made in a journey through the Western Counties of Scotland in the autumn of* 1792, Perth, 1793.


# Kirkcudbright, Kirkcudbrighshire

Here is a harbour without ships, a port without trade, a fishery without nets, a people without business; and, that which is worse than all, they do not seem to desire business, much less do they understand it.

DEFOE, D, *A tour thro' the whole Island of Great Britain*, London, 1727.

# Kirkwall, Orkney

The town of Kirkwall consists principally of one long street...
In most places it is narrow and dirty.

NEILL, P, *A Tour through some of the islands of Orkney and Shetland*,
Edinburgh, 1806.


# Lanark, Lanarkshire

A burgh town, but small, and ill built, and the inhabitants here
appear to be in a state of poverty.

THOMSON, W, *Tour in England and Scotland in 1785*,
London, 1788.

We got an indifferent dinner at the wretched
town of Lanark.

SKRINE, H, *Tours in the north of England and great part of Scotland*,
London, 1795.

We went directly to the first inn that presented itself to us...
We... were forthwith shown up into a large apartment upstairs...
the whole room exhibiting such marks of nastiness and filth as
would not easily be credited by those who have never seen any
excepting English inns... At length we obtained the scantiest
and the worst breakfast... during the whole of our route, were
obliged to pay double the sum that had hitherto been charged
for such a meal, and left the house.

BRISTED, J, *A Pedestrian Tour through part of the Highlands of Scotland in
1801*, London, 1803.

It is a dull, uninteresting place... The streets are narrow, dirty, and badly lighted.

CARTER, N, *Letters from Europe comprising The Journal of a Tour through... Scotland... in 1825*, New York, 1827.

## Black Bull Inn

We had no wish to enter the apartments; for it seemed the abode of dirt and poverty. The town - the doors and windows dirty, the shops dull, the women too seemed to be very dirty in their dress.

WORDSWORTH, D, *Recollections of a tour made in Scotland A.D. 1803.* Edinburgh, 1875.

## New Inn

The tables were un-wiped, chairs in disorder, the floor dirty, and the smell of liquors was most offensive.

WORDSWORTH, D, *Recollections of a tour made in Scotland A.D. 1803.* Edinburgh, 1875.

# Langholm, Dumfriesshire

The inn too bad to sleep at.

MURRAY, S, *A Companion and Useful Guide to the Beauties of Scotland*, London, 1799.

# Largo, Fife

To bed we went; the sheets were very coarse, tolerably clean, and immoderately damp, so that they clung fast to our limbs.

BRISTED, J, *A Pedestrian Tour through part of the Highlands of Scotland in 1801*, London, 1803.

# Lauder, Berwickshire

House only tolerable, which gave my friends but an indifferent opinion of Scotch accommodations.

THORNTON, T, *A Sporting Tour through the Northern parts of England and great part of the Highlands of Scotland*. London, 1804.

# Leith, Midlothian

The town is dirty and ill built, and chiefly inhabited by sailors.

PENNANT, T, *A Tour in Scotland 1769*, London, 1771.

Cowan now pointed out to me a woman walking into the sea, and, very deliberately, in full view of all those who were standing on the pier, pulling her vestments up above the middle of her waist, in order to cool and lave her limbs.

BRISTED, J, *A Pedestrian Tour through part of the Highlands of Scotland in 1801*, London, 1803.

The streets are narrow and dirty.

SILLIMAN, B, *A Journal of Travels in England, Holland and Scotland… in the years 1805 and 1806*, New York, 1810.

The entrance to Leith and the streets of Leith in general, are narrow and dirty. The fresh water of this town is very bad.

CARR, J, *Caledonian Sketches or A Tour through Scotland in 1807*, London, 1809.

At Dr D's, had some conversation on the cholera, which has appeared in the suburbs at the water of Leith. The people in that district as elsewhere, are much opposed to the hospitals, to which they will not consent to be removed; and to the physicians, whom they even abuse and pelt with mud and stones, fancying that they wish to destroy them for dissection.

MCLELLAN, H, *Journal of a Residence in Scotland*, Boston, 1834.

# Lerwick, Shetland

We had scarcely landed when some of the inhabitants asked of me - whether we were direct from Scotland? - a question that rather surprised me, as seeming to imply that the Shetland Islands themselves did not constitute a part of that country.

NEILL, P, *A Tour through some of the islands of Orkney and Shetland*, Edinburgh, 1806.

Happening to enter... a miserable bothie, or cottage, about two miles from Lerwick, I was surprised to observe an earthen ware tea-pot... simmering on a peat fire... Considering the indigestible and poor quality of their common food, (dried fish, often semi-putrescent, and coarse red cabbage), it is to be regretted that they are not encouraged to spent their scanty pittance of money on some more substantial and nutritive delicacy.

NEILL, P, *A Tour through some of the islands of Orkney and Shetland*, Edinburgh, 1806.

# Letter Finlay, Inverness-shire

Its considerable structure, when compared with the huts of the country, and its newly whitened front, made us expect better fare that we had hitherto found in the Highland inns; but words are not equal to describe the squalid appearance of filth, misery, and poverty, which prevailed within, and surrounded us while we hurried through our homely dinner with no small portion of disgust.

SKRINE, H, *Tours in the north of England and great part of Scotland*, London, 1795.

Letterfinlay is a solitary inn, as dirty and miserable as any venta in Spain; and worse, with regard to cleanliness and accommodation, than any other in Scotland that I met with.

CARR, J, *Caledonian Sketches or A Tour through Scotland in* 1807, London, 1809.

The worst shelter for poor travellers I have ever been in.

COCKBURN, H, *Circuit Journeys by the late Lord Cockburn*, Edinburgh, 1889.

Halted at Letter Finlay, a single house, which is said to have been much improved of late; it is not easy to believe that it can ever have been dirtier than it is now.

SOUTHEY, R, *Journal of a tour in Scotland in* 1819, London, 1929.

# Linlithgow, West Lothian

A poor but not very small town.

LONDONER, *North of England and Scotland in* 1704, Edinburgh, 1818.

The town decayed, dirty, and dolorous.
SOUTHEY, R, *Journal of a tour in Scotland in* 1819, London, 1929.

# Isle of Lismore, Argyllshire

This island is one of the principal seats of illicit distillation.
BOTFIELD, B, *Journal of a Tour Through the Highlands of Scotland during the Summer of* 1829, Edinburgh, 1830.

# Little Loch Broom, Ross and Cromarty

Little Loch Broom is utterly without interest.
MacCULLOCH, J *The Highlands and Western Isles of Scotland*, London, 1824.

# Loch Achray, Perthshire
## Ardchincrocan Inn

One may lawfully vent one's spleen upon the fecklessness of the head waiter... The creature regularly supplied the teapot with cold water, never brought a thing one asked for, and his dry toast was as hard as tiles... I... have been writing in a small double bedded room a trifle fresher than the Black Hole of Calcutta.
TOWNSHEND, C, *A Descriptive Tour of Scotland*, London, 1840.

# Lochaline, Argyllshire

After passing Lochaline Castle... we observed nothing note-
worthy, with the exception of the huts of the poor people,
which come nearer to vegetable productions than to human
habitations, their walls being entirely composed of living turf.

TOWNSHEND, C, *A Descriptive Tour of Scotland*, London, 1840.

# Loch Arkaig, by Fort William, Inverness-shire

The owner of this lake, and the whole beautiful country round,
is a poor creature wholly unworthy of his fortune... The estate is
in the hands of trustees, and he lives miserably in London upon
£600 a year, kept needy by his debauched course of life, and
eking out his pittance by cutting down his woods.

SOUTHEY, R, *Journal of a tour in Scotland in 1819*, London, 1929.

# Loch Broom, Ross and Cromarty

We had anchored in this inlet; and, in the night, I was roused
by a great weight, tumbling, with vast commotion and outrage,
into my berth... I put out my hand in some alarm, and laid
hold of a pair of horns... It proved to be a goat, which the
men had brought on board that we might be sure of milk for
our breakfasts. Unluckily, when it came to be milked, it was
discovered to be a he goat.

MacCULLOCH, J *The Highlands and Western Isles of Scotland*,
London, 1824.

# Lochcarron, Ross and Cromarty

We had been told that the inn here was very superior. But it is just a good bad inn.

COCKBURN, H, *Circuit Journeys by the late Lord Cockburn*, Edinburgh, 1889.

We took up our night's abode at Jean-town... Our sitting room is larger than seems either needful or comfortable in such a situation, and there is no air of neatness about it.

SOUTHEY, R, *Journal of a tour in Scotland in 1819*, London, 1929.

# Loch Fyne, Argyllshire

I know no term by which I can so well characterize the style of Loch Fyne from Cairndow to Inverary, as meanness... the hills are rude and bare. Even rudeness and bareness may however be beautiful... but there are no such redeeming beauties here.

MacCULLOCH, J *The Highlands and Western Isles of Scotland*, London, 1824.

## Cairndow Inn

Cairndow. A very indifferent inn.

THOMSON, W, *Tour in England and Scotland in 1785*, London, 1788.

We returned to Cairndow, where an abundant dinner was prepared for us, greasily cooked, and served much after the fashion of a ship's mess. But by this time we had so much overcome the fastidious recollection of southern taste and manners, as to be easily pleased with our food, and perfectly reconciled to bare legs and feet. If our Ganymede was a little dirty boy, or if our Hebe served us with coarse and filthy hands, arms and face, we regarded them equally with the utmost indifference.

MAWMAN, J, *An Excursion to the Highlands of Scotland and the English Lakes*, London, 1805.

# Loch Katrine, Perthshire

The term RAIN is not at all applicable to this kind of aqueous precipitation. We seemed to have got entangled in the tail of a water spout... In the Highlands of Scotland, more than in any mountainous country with which I am acquainted, a Mackintosh Waterproof Cloak is peculiarly useful. There is often no time to unfold, much less to unbutton an umbrella; for while the sun is shining full in our faces, and scarcely a cloud to be seen, twenty buckets of water are dashed on our heads, without the admonition of a sprinkling, or even a harbinger drop.

JOHNSON, J, *The Recess or Autumnal relaxations in the Highlands and Lowlands*, London, 1834.

The road was said to be good, the meaning of which we found to be that it was practicable for a coach, being in reality not only very bad, but in no slight degree dangerous.

SOUTHEY, R, *Journal of a tour in Scotland in 1819*, London, 1929.

# Loch Linnhe, Argyllshire

From Portnacroish, we continued for some distance along the shore of Loch Linnhe, and by a winding pass through the mountains to Ballachulish ferry on Loch Leven... During this part of the journey we passed through several of the poorer sort of villages, than which it would be difficult to find more wretched collections of hovels. We could scarcely believe that human beings could submit, contentedly to occupy dwellings so deficient in comfort and cleanliness, let alone live cheerfully in such filthy abodes.

PEDESTRIAN, *A six weeks' tour in the Highlands of Scotland*, London, 1851.

# Loch Lomond

The blind fiddler... who was also on board, was a mitigated nuisance; but the bagpiper was an unmitigated evil, and never ought to have been permitted to walk the deck... The discordant noises that our Loch Lomond piper produced from his ear splitting apparatus were a real detraction to the enjoyment of the scene... We have very many things to be thankful for in England in the nineteenth century, and, among others, that the good old days are past and gone when the bagpipes were common throughout the land... We too, may rest at the comfortable hotel, and be thankful that the bagpiper is severed from us, we trust, forever. Alas, for the vanity of human wishes. While we are looking out of window... a wild yell, as from a hundred tortured pigs, ascends upon the breeze, and there... pacing the lawn in front of the hotel is the wretched man with the baggy-pipe.

BEDE, C, *A Tour in Tartan-Land*, London, 1863.

# The Lowlands

The common people of Scotland are more than a century behind the English in improvement; and the manners of the Lowlanders in particular cannot fail to disgust a stranger. All the stories that are propagated of the filth and habitual dirtiness of this people are surpassed by the reality; and the squalid unwholesome appearance of their garb and countenances, is exceeded by the wretchedness that prevails within their houses. Their manners are equally unpleasant, being uncommunicative and forbidding in the extreme; and whole groups of villagers fly from the approach of a traveller, like the most untamed of savages... The Highlanders – a manly, bold, and hardy race, are courteous in their manners, civil in their address, and hospitable to the utmost extent of their little power. Their houses, it is true, are mean and inconsiderable; but within they are often as clean as their poverty will allow; and their doors are never closed against the necessities or curiosity of a stranger.

SKRINE, H, *Tours in the north of England and great part of Scotland*, London, 1795.

I had little reason to complain of my entertainment at the several houses where I set up, because I never wanted what was proper for the support of life... the worst of all was the cookery... The little fishing towns were generally disagreeable to pass, from the strong smell of the haddocks and whitings that were hung up to dry on lines along the sides of the houses.

BURT, E & JAMIESON, R, *Letters from a Gentleman in the North of Scotland to his friend in London*, London, 1818.

# Lochmaben, Dumfriesshire

Contrary to our expectation, we have found a decent hostelry in
this wretched carcass of a royal burgh.

COCKBURN, H, *Circuit Journeys by the late Lord Cockburn*,
Edinburgh, 1889.

# Lochmaddy, North Uist, Outer Hebrides

There is one advantage in a shower in this country, that you
are not kept waiting in fretful expectation, wondering how
long it will be before you are wet through. The business is
completed in five minutes.

MacCULLOCH, J *The Highlands and Western Isles of Scotland*,
London, 1824.

As a general rule, a more utterly lonely spot could scarcely be
found than this flat dull shore.

GORDON-CUMMING, C, *From the Hebrides to the Himalayas*,
London, 1876.

# Loch Maree, Ross and Cromarty

In point of style, it ranks rather more nearly with Loch
Lomond than with any other of the southern lakes; though
still very far inferior.

MacCULLOCH, J *The Highlands and Western Isles of Scotland*,
London, 1824.

In general, people prefer sailing down Loch Maree to walking along either of its banks, and a boat can always be hired for any distance at the rate of a shilling a mile and a bottle of whisky for the whole voyage.

ANDERSON, G & ANDERSON, P, *Guide to the Highlands and Islands of Scotland*, London, 1834.

# Loch Ness, Inverness-shire

The water is said to be unwholesome, acting as a purgative upon man and beast.

SOUTHEY, R, *Journal of a tour in Scotland in 1819*, London, 1929.

## Paddle Steamer Comet

At 6 o'clock we embarked, with between one and two hundred others, on board the steam boat Comet... To persons accustomed to the splendid accommodations and the sumptuous tables on board of an American steam boat, the contracted size and wretched fare of the Comet afforded but a sad specimen of the little progress, which Europe has yet made in this mode of travelling... the boats are too small: they are apparently constructed in the worst possible manner, both for speed and comfort: the officers make bungling work in guiding them: and coarse provisions are badly cooked... Such a multitude... furnished an excellent opportunity for studying the dress, manners, and habits of the Highlanders... When a circle of half a dozen gathered round a table, and for hours drank whisky punch, till their cheeks became flushed and their eyes dim, the scene was too clearly proved, that they had not forgotten their fondness for the bottle. So far as I have observed, a love of whisky is universal among the lower classes in Scotland. Both sexes will take it in any and every shape, and in immeasurable quantities. It is as much a national drink, as beer is in England, but has a very different effect upon the constitution, producing when taken to excess, thin, emaciated forms, with sallow, smoky countenances, instead of the rotundity and rosy complexion of the English.

CARTER, N, *Letters from Europe comprising The Journal of a Tour through... Scotland... in 1825*, New York, 1827.

{The Comet, on a trip shortly thereafter, collided with another steamer off Gourock in the Firth of Clyde and sank with the loss of over 60 lives.}

# Loch Oich, Inverness-shire

Long before Loch Oich was skirted, our situation had become deplorable, owing to the deluges incessantly pouring from the merciless skies. A wretched cabin, where whisky was sold, at length presented itself... Had the hovel been aught superior to a pig sty, we would have thankfully accepted the shelter it offered; but smoke, filth, and the pestilential odour arising from a crowd of bipeds and quadrupeds stowed promiscuously into one common apartment, were too great plagues to submit to... The motley group in this hovel were comforting themselves with the worst whisky we tasted in the Highlands.

SUTHERLAND, A, *A Summer Ramble in the North Highlands*, Edinburgh, 1825.

# Loch Tay, Perthshire

Though Loch Tay is a spacious and splendid piece of water... it scarcely affords one landscape from Kenmore to near Killin; nor do I know any place in Scotland which, with so much promise, produces so much disappointment.

MacCULLOCH, J *The Highlands and Western Isles of Scotland*,
London, 1824.

To add to our blisses, came a sudden flaw of rain, against which our umbrella was rather less useful than it might have been against a mad bull.

TOWNSHEND, C, *A Descriptive Tour of Scotland*, London, 1840.

# Lockerbie, Dumfriesshire

A very bad inn.

MURRAY, S, *A Companion and Useful Guide to the Beauties of Scotland*,
London, 1799.

The room wherein I were to lay was overflown with water, so that the people laid heaps of turf for me to tread on to get from the door to the fireplace... The floor was so worn in holes that had I tread aside a turf, I might have sunk up to my knees in mud and water, and no better room was to be had in this town... My room had but half a door, and that to the street, and the wall was broke down between the stable and me, so that the room lay open to the stable.

LONDONER, *North of England and Scotland in* 1704,
Edinburgh, 1818.

# Luib, by Achnasheen, Ross and Cromarty

Stopped at Luib, a house one degree better that the hovel at Achanalt... One end of the room contained three beds like ship cabins, each shut in with folding doors... They may be clean; but they must be close, and are evidently unfavourable to cleanliness, a virtue in which the Scotch are notoriously wanting.

SOUTHEY, R, *Journal of a tour in Scotland in* 1819, London, 1929.

# Luss, Dunbartonshire

We found our bowels so dolefully twisted and tormented by the sorry and uncertain diet by which we had fed, that I told Cowan we were now in a proper state to become the disciples... of St Jerome, who strenuously recommends abstinence.

BRISTED, J, *A Pedestrian Tour through part of the Highlands of Scotland in* 1801, London, 1803.

We now began to find that we were leaving the land of the kilt, and entering upon a country of breeches... from the very different mode of reception which we experienced. The Highlanders, for the most part, had been open, unsuspecting, kind, and hospitable; but in general the Lowlanders received us with coldness and suspicion, hesitatingly, and often unkindly.

BRISTED, J, *A Pedestrian Tour through part of the Highlands of Scotland in* 1801, London, 1803.

One of the houses... we entered... It contained two slovenly young women, who were sitting idly near the glowing embers, enjoying the comforts of smarting eyes and suffocation, though the pure air and summer sun were to be enjoyed on the outside of their habitation... We visited another dwelling, which was somewhat larger, and much neater. Its possessor was the wife of a servant of Sir James Colquhoun... She had learnt, in respectable families, the divine habits of cleanliness and industry.

MAWMAN, J, *An Excursion to the Highlands of Scotland and the English Lakes*, London, 1805.

The church of Luss... is beautiful as ever, but the dirt and squalid wretchedness of the houses and people of that village is a disgrace to the landlords.

COCKBURN, H, *Circuit Journeys by the late Lord Cockburn*, Edinburgh, 1889.

## Luss Inn

There is an inn [Tarbet], much better and cleaner then that at Luss.

THOMSON, W, *Tour in England and Scotland in* 1785, London, 1788.

We journeyed on in ceaseless admiration till we came to our appointed Inn, which we found very unsuitable to the merits of so bewitching a situation, and by much the worst we had met with in our tour. It was a small inconvenient building, with bad provisions, and dirty attendance, nay, even destitute of the means of furnishing its guests with wheat bread, which we had precaution enough to carry with us.

SHAW, S, *A Tour, in 1787, from London to the Western Highlands of Scotland*, London, 1788.

A sad noisy, strapping, blustering wench waited upon us... after banging the door every time she went out of the room, with a noise resembling thunder, and by an unlucky bounce of by far the largest member of her body... brought us some excellent tart and mutton, which should have been eaten, could it ever have been swallowed, at least a week before we had the misfortune to have more than one sense disgusted by its presence; vile, filthy water, tolerable porter, good butter and cheese, and the dirtiest table cloth that ever mortal eyes beheld.

BRISTED, J, *A Pedestrian Tour through part of the Highlands of Scotland in 1801*, London, 1803.

After a short walk... came to the inn, which I hoped to have found much improved... but cannot say I found the difference here I had expected... The stables were not divided, the hay bad, but little straw, and no coach house. All this I guessed would happen very soon, but not at Luss.

THORNTON, T, *A Sporting Tour through the Northern parts of England and great part of the Highlands of Scotland*. London, 1804.

At Luss, you wait four hours for your dinner... and if there be any bread, you have devoured it all before the dinner arrives. When it does, it consists of herrings which might

have been cooked in ten minutes, and of mutton which
was cooked yesterday.

MacCULLOCH, J *The Highlands and Western Isles of Scotland*,
London, 1824.

The house was clean for a Scotch inn... We had a poor dinner,
and sour ale... The girl brought in the tea things, but no fire,
and when I asked if she was coming to light it, she said 'her
mistress was not very willing to give fire.' I had seen the
landlady... her countenance corresponded with the unkindness
of allowing us a fire on a cold night, for she was the most cruel
and hateful looking woman I ever saw. She was overgrown with
fat, and was sitting with her feet and legs in a tub of water for the
dropsy – probably brought on by whisky drinking... William and
Coleridge had bad beds, in a two bedded room in the garrets,
though there were empty rooms on the first floor, and they
were disturbed by a drunken man, who had come to the inn
when we were gone to sleep.

WORDSWORTH, D, *Recollections of a tour made in Scotland
A.D.* 1803. Edinburgh, 1875.

# Lybster, Caithness

Near Lybster, a troop of females passed us, each carrying on
her back a heavy creel filled with rotten moss, which is also
employed as manure. This mode of carriage seemed somewhat
barbarous, particularly as droves of dwarf horses... usually hop
in idleness over the adjacent commons.

SUTHERLAND, A, *A Summer Ramble in the North Highlands*,
Edinburgh, 1825.

# Melrose, Roxburghshire

There is nothing in the town worth seeing.

CARR, J, *Caledonian Sketches or A Tour through Scotland in 1807*,
London, 1809.

The Tweed takes a noble sweep, encircling the town of Melrose,
the paltry streets of which sadly detract from the picturesque
appearance of the abbey.

BOTFIELD, B, *Journal of a Tour Through the Highlands of Scotland during
the Summer of 1829*, Edinburgh, 1830.

# Midlothian

At length, a large shaggy cur, after investigating me for about
half a minute, and not finding that I moved, for I was too debile
to make any exertion... seized hold of my neck cloth and jacket
collar with his teeth, and, when I put up my hand, very feebly...
the beast relinquished his hold, it is true; but, in order to show
his utter contempt for me, he lifted up his hinder leg and
founted all over the middle of my body.

BRISTED, J, *A Pedestrian Tour through part of the Highlands of Scotland in
1801*, London, 1803.

## Middleton Inn

That nasty little alehouse.

COCKBURN, H, *Circuit Journeys by the late Lord Cockburn*,
Edinburgh, 1889.

# Moffat, Dumfriesshire

Moffat is but a small town, noted for its medicinal well... the water tastes like rotten eggs, or rather like the washings of a gun barrel... The waters are said to purge and vomit, and are mightily esteemed against colicky and nephritical disorders, powerfully removing obstructions in the bowels.

VOLUNTEER, *A Journey through part of England and Scotland... in the year* 1746, London, 1747.

In summer time, people come here to drink waters... but where they get lodgings I can't tell, for I did not like their lodgings well enough to go to bed.

LONDONER, *North of England and Scotland in* 1704, Edinburgh, 1818.

# Moniaive, Dumfriesshire

A wretched, half dead village.

COCKBURN, H, *Circuit Journeys by the late Lord Cockburn*, Edinburgh, 1889.

# Morvern Peninsula, Argyllshire

The interior country from Strontian to Ardnamurchan Point, is mountainous, bare, and wild; and utterly without interest unless when we approximate to the sea shores.

MacCULLOCH, J *The Highlands and Western Isles of Scotland*, London, 1824.

# Moulinearn, by Ballinluig, Perthshire

About six o'clock in the evening arrived at the halfway inn between Dunkeld and Blair Atholl... and kept by a Madam Pennycook, whose flat, fat, bloated carcase, and brandy drinking face, betokening all the petty malignancy of supercilious ignorance, we did not much relish... We were shown into a little, vile, unholy, dirty room, upstairs... But, to our great astonishment, we found that the benevolent and lovely hostess would, on no account, suffer us to sleep in her house... After much time spent in discourse, this amiable woman... graciously condescended to let us sleep in an outhouse at some distance from the inn... To this dormitory we were conducted by... the landlady's own son... in whom the beauty of the baboon was united with the wisdom of the ass... It was a small room with a dirt floor... In a corner lay our bed... the linen was so marvellously foul and filthy that I asked the good Mr Pennycook whether he ought not to be ashamed even to think of putting a dog into such a vile dirty hole. His answer was - that I need not make such a noise about it; that the sheets were pretty cleanish, for that only two foot passengers and a carrier had slept in them since they were last washed.

BRISTED, J, *A Pedestrian Tour through part of the Highlands of Scotland in 1801*, London, 1803.

# Musselburgh, Midlothian

We next came to Musselburgh... Here the scene was the same over again at Haddington, where the women were extreme ugly and nasty, having dirty clouts tied round their heads, falling about their shoulders, and peeping out of pieces of boarded windows, just big enough for the size of their head; they put me in mind of pigeon holes... Their butter is loathsome to both eye and taste... The nastiness of their food, together with their dirty beds, makes me always in fear of either a surfeit, or itch.

VOLUNTEER, *A Journey through part of England and Scotland... in the year 1746*, London, 1747.

A small, poor town.

LONDONER, *North of England and Scotland in 1704*, Edinburgh, 1818.

## Fisherrow

Squalid houses and dirty exterior.

BEDE, C, *A Tour in Tartan-Land*, London, 1863.

# Nairn, Nairnshire

The north east end of the town is composed of miserable mountain huts.

THOMSON, W, *Tour in England and Scotland in 1785*, London, 1788.

As to Nairn, what can I say. They build ships in ditches in the sand, and cut them out when ready. Part of the people speak Gaelic, and the rest English, because it is the Highland boundary. The baker and the brewer are not so rich as at Inverness, and the attorney, being poorer, is probably a greater rogue. Those who trust to the apothecary, die of him, here as elsewhere; the old maids abuse their neighbours; and those who have the misfortune to come into the town, get out of it again as fast as they can.

MacCULLOCH, J *The Highlands and Western Isles of Scotland*,
London, 1824.

Ill paved, straggling, little sea port.

BOTFIELD, B, *Journal of a Tour Through the Highlands of Scotland during
the Summer of* 1829,
Edinburgh, 1830.

Bleak and exposed, and seemingly dead.

COCKBURN, H, *Circuit Journeys by the late Lord Cockburn*,
Edinburgh, 1889.

# Nethy Bridge, Inverness-shire

Where there is a miserable house of refreshment.

ANDERSON, G & ANDERSON, P, *Guide to the Highlands and Islands of
Scotland*, London, 1834.

# North Kessock, Ross and Cromarty

The ferryman had entrusted it to a boy, who, with two or three companions, yet greener in years, were amusing themselves by paddling round the pier head... During the whole passage, a sun tanned, bonnet-less urchin, in a ragged kilt, sat with his naked foot stuffed into a large hole in the bottom of the boat... we were in water to the ankles ere we reached the opposite shore. Here the lazy boatmen were discovered comfortably asleep on the grass; and, when we remonstrated with them on the impropriety of leaving their duty to be discharged by a child, they very independently saluted us with a volley of abusive language.

SUTHERLAND, A, *A Summer Ramble in the North Highlands*, Edinburgh, 1825.

# North Ronaldsay, Orkney

North Ronaldsay, the most northerly of the Orkneys, and from which Fair Isle may be seen in a clear day, belongs to Mr Traill of Woodwick, whose tenants, the natives, are considered more primitive in their manners than those of any other part of Orkney.

ANDERSON, G & ANDERSON, P, *Guide to the Highlands and Islands of Scotland*, London, 1834.

# North Uist, Outer Hebrides

All the east coast of North Uist is the same sort of dreary, boggy, mossy, peaty soil, with weary, uninteresting, low creeks and inlets.

GORDON-CUMMING, C, *From the Hebrides to the Himalayas*, London, 1876.

# Oldmeldrum, Aberdeenshire

Oldmeldrum is a dull and insignificant village... and has neither antiquity not modern neatness to recommend it.

SUTHERLAND, A, *A Summer Ramble in the North Highlands*, Edinburgh, 1825.

# Orkney

The ferries of Orkney are under no regulation. Often the boats, and still oftener the boatmen, are of the worst kind. Yet they charge on a stranger very high fares. Indeed they exercise very generally a low cunning if they discover that their employer is unacquainted with the customary dues, they rise in their demand, telling perhaps abundance of soothing lies, to make their extortion less unpalatable.

NEILL, P, *A Tour through some of the islands of Orkney and Shetland*, Edinburgh, 1806.

It is a shame... that the clergy in the Shetland and Orkney Islands should so often wink at their churches being the repositories of smuggled goods, chiefly foreign spirits.
The apostle Paul exhorts his converts not to be filled with wine, wherein is excess, but to be filled with the spirit.
The people in the Orkney and Shetland Islands, perhaps, misinterpret this text.

HALL, J, *Travels in Scotland by an unusual route*, London, 1807.

The population has, however, a very primitive appearance.

WELD, C, *Two months in the Highlands, Orcadia, and Skye*, London, 1860.

# Outer Hebrides

On our return to the hotel, we had the satisfaction to find our New England friends. They gave frightful accounts... of their own adventures, upon the western coast of Scotland... A part of their voyage among the Hebrides was performed in an open cock-boat, exposed to the united violence of wind and waves, with a crew who were willing to risk life for money, and whose native temerity was increased by liberal potations of whisky. Wo betide the traveller, who too late finds his mistake in having committed himself to such hands.

CARTER, N, *Letters from Europe comprising The Journal of a Tour through... Scotland... in 1825*, New York, 1827.

We were delighted to hear that the very obvious plan of improving the unenclosed commons, is about to be tried on a great scale by Colonel Gordon of Cluny, who lately purchased a large estate on 'the Long Island,' which is chiefly distinguished for being the ugliest place in Scotland.

SINCLAIR, C, *Scotland and the Scotch*, New York, 1840.

We wish to hold out a helping hand, to assist in raising these people from a slough of ignorance, dishonesty, superstition, and filth, as shameful, and degrading, and as unwarrantable and unjustifiable as any that ever shocked a philanthropist.

GRAY, T, *Barra, in the Outer Hebrides*, Nature and Art, Vol. 1, London, 1866.

The people here {North Uist} at once strike the visitor as being more cleanly and intelligent than their neighbours.

GRAY, T, *Barra, in the Outer Hebrides*, Nature and Art, Vol. 1, London, 1866.

In the six months ending June 1866, very nearly £300,000 worth of property has been washed ashore, or has appeared in distress off these islands... but the islanders look upon these wrecks as a special dispensation of a wise Providence... Perhaps the worst feature of all was the way in which the survivors are reported to have been treated; they were, as was stated in the press truthfully, in many instances pitilessly plundered by the cottars of what little they had contrived to save and bring ashore.

GRAY, T, *Barra, in the Outer Hebrides*, Nature and Art, Vol. 1, London, 1866.

# Paisley, Renfrewshire

Its streets disappointed me, exhibiting a bad miniature of the superior grandeur of Glasgow, but without its beauty or regularity.

SKRINE, H, *Tours in the north of England and great part of Scotland*, London, 1795.

# Papa Stour, Shetland

The tourist... should not omit paying a visit to its grand porphyritic stacks, and magnificent underground rocky excavations, which the inhabitants visit at certain seasons armed with thick clubs, and well provided with candles, in search of the seals which breed in them.

ANDERSON, G & ANDERSON, P, *Guide to the Highlands and Islands of Scotland*, London, 1834.

# Papa Westray, Orkney

In this sequestered spot, the total want of competition seems, however, to shed a languor over all the motions of the inhabitants. In their work, they exhibit a dullness and slowness which form a perfect contrast with the activity of most servants in the south.

NEILL, P, *A Tour through some of the islands of Orkney and Shetland*, Edinburgh, 1806.

# Perth, Perthshire

The two principal and most esteemed national games in Scotland are curling and golf. The former is, of the two, the most distinguished and interesting... The reader will not be a little surprised when he learns that the whole game of golf consists of nothing more than how to drive, with a stick, and with the fewest possible number of strokes, a little hard ball, into a hole placed at a very great distance.

KOHL, J, *Travels in Scotland*, London, 1849.

# Perthshire

The peasantry... some still speak the Gaelic language... In the wilder parts, they live still much upon milk, and upon the carcasses of sheep which have died by accident or by disease. In addition to their milk, they make free use of whisky. The shepherds are averse from all labour, save merely that which is unavoidably exacted from them in then tending of their flocks.

HERON, R, *Observations made in a journey through the Western Counties of Scotland in the autumn of* 1792, Perth, 1793.

# Peterhead, Aberdeenshire

At Peterhead is a very good mineral spring, which is considered as very efficacious in removing any complaint in the bowels.

THOMSON, W, *Tour in England and Scotland in* 1785, London, 1788.

The accommodation was superior to what I could expect in so remote a spot, and a spirit of neatness and civility prevailing throughout, formed a strong contrast to the general dirtiness of the towns of Scotland, and the coarseness of their inhabitants.

SKRINE, H, *Tours in the north of England and great part of Scotland*, London, 1795.

# Pitkeathly Wells, Bridge of Earn, Perthshire

Though I have drunk copiously of the waters of Bath,
Cheltenham, &c. without feeling any effect from them, yet,
I confess, the water of Pitkeathly made me drink with caution...
The morning after my arrival, having drunk a pint of the
waters, I strolled about before breakfast, reflecting on the
indelicacy of both men and women, almost everywhere, in sight
of one another, running constantly behind bushes and hedges:
but it was not long before I completely sympathised with them...
I tried what effect the water would have on my horse; and
from what I observed, perceived that it had the same effect on
quadrupeds as on bipeds.

HALL, J, *Travels in Scotland by an unusual route*, London, 1807.

# Portnacroish, Appin, Argyllshire

At Portnacroish... our miserable plight compelled us to stop,
although the accommodations were very indifferent. Our
bedroom was a small confined apartment, without a carpet, and
the partition from the adjoining room was composed of boards
set upright, at such a respectable distance from each other, that
we could not only hear, but see all that passed therein; and what
was worse, were placed under similar surveillance ourselves.
In the room below a party of gruff Highlanders, drinking and
singing Gaelic songs at the top of their voices, alarmed us not
a little, as we took it into our heads, from their coarse and

fancied villainous looking countenances, they were a party
of Highland banditti.

PEDESTRIAN, *A six weeks' tour in the Highlands of Scotland*,
London, 1851.

It is a small village, a few huts and an indifferent inn by the side
of the loch... Had an indifferent dinner.

WORDSWORTH, D, *Recollections of a tour made in Scotland
A.D. 1803*. Edinburgh, 1875.

# Portpatrick, Wigtownshire

Portpatrick has nothing in it to invite our stay, 'tis a mean dirty
homely place; and as we had no business here, but to see the
coast, we came away very ill satisfied with our accommodations.

DEFOE, D, *A tour thro' the whole Island of Great Britain*, London, 1727.

# Portsoy, Banffshire

Portsoy... has neither commercial importance not beauty of
site to recommend it.

SUTHERLAND, A, *A Summer Ramble in the North Highlands*,
Edinburgh, 1825.

# Rhiconich, Sutherland

At the head of this bay, in cheerless solitude, stands the little
inn, by no means a good specimen of the 'Dukes Houses.'

Indeed, so exceptionally bad is it, that had I not been very tired, I would have pushed on to Scourie.

WELD, C, *Two months in the Highlands, Orcadia, and Skye*, London, 1860.

# Rothesay, Isle of Bute, County of Bute

The architecture is in different styles of ugliness, but all as frightful as stone and lime can make them.

SINCLAIR, C, *Scotland and the Scotch*, New York, 1840.

# Sanquhar, Dumfriesshire

As the rain now began greatly to increase, I betook myself for shelter under a neighbouring hut, where I was early introduced into a scene of apparent wretchedness which ocular demonstration only can make one believe. This was surely more than anticipation of Highland poverty, and might vie with the most recluse parts of the Hebrides. But what afforded me some degree of pleasure, and reconciled my feelings to the scene, was the cheerfulness that smiled around the owners of this dismal hut, even amidst the depressing circumstances of sickness, pain, and want.

SHAW, S, *A Tour, in 1787, from London to the Western Highlands of Scotland*, London, 1788.

Oat straw was our sheets, and port-mantles our pillows... The next day we recruited with some country ale, but so thick and ropey it was, that you might eat it with spoons.

Besides, some small quantity of cooking was brought us, enough to discover the cookery of the country; and the linen they supplied us with, were it not to boast of, was little or nothing different from those female complexions that never washed their faces... In every house, fowl women, fowl linen and fowl pewter.

FRANCK, R, *Northern Memoirs calculated for the Meridian of Scotland... writ in the year* 1658, Edinburgh, 1821.

# Selkirk, Selkirkshire

Nothing can be more deplorable than its appearance. The houses are mostly old, falling to pieces, and deserted: nothing but dirt and misery to be seen. I had not breakfasted, therefore entered the inn; and being, at that time, an inexperienced traveller, I was totally un-provided with necessaries for that meal. Every being, and thing in the house, disgusted me at first sight; the extreme dirt, and the smell of the whole, was nauseating in the highest degree. The inn is too bad, either to eat or sleep at.

MURRAY, S, *A Companion and Useful Guide to the Beauties of Scotland*, London, 1799.

## Sir Walter Scott Statue

A sad piece of sculpture, not very honourable to the gentry of Selkirkshire.

COCKBURN, H, *Circuit Journeys by the late Lord Cockburn*, Edinburgh, 1889.

# Shapinsay, Orkney

Shapinsay is a wet island, and contains nothing to interest the traveller.

ANDERSON, G & ANDERSON, P, *Guide to the Highlands and Islands of Scotland*, London, 1834.

# Shetland

The greater part of the Shetland tenants appeared to me to be sunk into a state of the most abject poverty and misery. I found them even without bread; without any kind of food, in short, but fish and cabbage; living, in many cases, under the same roof with their cattle.

NEILL, P, *A Tour through some of the islands of Orkney and Shetland*, Edinburgh, 1806.

Trees – there are none in Shetland. Shetlanders who have never been from home have no idea of trees.

NEILL, P, *A Tour through some of the islands of Orkney and Shetland*, Edinburgh, 1806.

I formerly remarked, that there were no Justices of the Peace in Shetland. I am happy to hear that two gentlemen have lately qualified. At their first sessions, above a hundred delinquents, it is said, were convened before them, chiefly, however, for making malt in private.

NEILL, P, *A Tour through some of the islands of Orkney and Shetland*, Edinburgh, 1806.

Their speech, indeed, is not intelligible to a stranger until he has heard it for some months... The lower ranks are dirty in their clothes and persons; and their houses are low,

SCOTLAND THE WORST

damp, smoky huts, which they inhabit in common with their cattle. It is likewise to be regretted, that they discover a great partiality for spirituous liquors, and seldom fail to indulge in them to excess when they can procure them... The common people of Shetland, like those of more polished countries, are too much inclined to plunder the property of the shipwrecked.

HALL, J, *Travels in Scotland by an unusual route*, London, 1807.

# Shiel Bridge, Ross and Cromarty
## Shiel Bridge Inn

Mere drovers' quarters, and bad quarters for the poorest drovers.

COCKBURN, H, *Circuit Journeys by the late Lord Cockburn*, Edinburgh, 1889.

# Solway Firth, Kirkcudbrightshire

I had been told (but only by Galwegians) to expect something uncommonly fine along this part of the shores of the Solway, and from this highway. I was disappointed. It is the stupidest of all our Firths.

COCKBURN, H, *Circuit Journeys by the late Lord Cockburn*, Edinburgh, 1889.

# South Creagan, Argyllshire

We found only women at home in the ferry house... the house was so dirty, and there were so many wretchedly dirty women and children: yet perhaps I might have got over the dirt, though I believe there are few ladies who would not have been turned sick by it, if there had not been a most disgusting combination of laziness and coarseness in the countenances and manners of the women.

WORDSWORTH, D, *Recollections of a tour made in Scotland A.D.* 1803. Edinburgh, 1875.

# South Uist, Outer Hebrides

Of all the Hebrideans, these highlanders are the wildest, and civilisation appears to have made but little progress among them... The women wear the ancient costume. Their feet and knees are naked, and the calves of their legs are covered with pieces of grey woollen stockings. The women of South Uist have not however a single fine feature; their coarse faces appear discoloured by labour, whilst the greater part wear their fat and greasy hair hanging in long bunches over their foreheads and shoulders... The lower class of Highlanders are generally ugly. Those of the higher classes, particularly the females, in the beauty of their figure and complexion present a striking contrast to the ugliness of the peasants.

DE SAUSSURE, L, *A Voyage to the Hebrides*, London, 1822.

SCOTLAND THE WORST

At the inn at Polochar, South Uist, there are four rooms on a floor: one was the tap room, another was the stable and cow house, a third a pigsty, and the fourth a sort of dung heap... In truth, the inns have not been run down enough: they are execrable holes.

GRAY, T, *Barra, in the Outer Hebrides*, Nature and Art, Vol. 1, London, 1866.

Dreary and desolate as are the low shores of Benbecula, South Uist is more dreary and desolate still... Such miserable human beings as have settled on this side of the island are said to be poorer and more wretched, their hovels more squalid, their filth more unavoidable than any others in the isles... The people {of Barra} are generally a cheerful race – very different from the dwellers in the bogs of South Uist.

GORDON-CUMMING, C, *From the Hebrides to the Himalayas*, London, 1876.

# Spittal of Glenshee, Perthshire

We reached a lonely inn called the Spittal... of Glenshee. The hospitality of the hospice was, however, somewhat of a dubious kind. How could landlord and waiters attend to us... seeing that Lord Rokeby and a crowd of sportsmen had just arrived... We were crammed into a sort of pantry, where, had we stayed at the Spittal, we should have had to sleep.

TOWNSHEND, C, *A Descriptive Tour of Scotland*, London, 1840.

# St Andrews, Fife

The great street of St Andrews presents on either hand a
melancholy scene of stately houses either falling down and
dilapidated, or degraded to meaner purposes then those for
which they were originally designed. The building of its colleges
too, are greatly decayed.

HERON, R, *Observations made in a journey through the Western Counties of
Scotland in the autumn of* 1792, Perth, 1793.

We entered the first public house that we saw, and were
shown into a small room, containing literally a chair
and a half, and no table. Here we waited awhile, till the
landlord, a large, fat, unwieldy, surly looking fellow...
wearing a brown wig and a forbidding scowl, came into
the room. He surveyed us and our knapsacks with great
contempt, and told us, with some asperity, that we should
have no lodging in his house, and must seek further... At
the next receptacle of travellers an old dirty woman, with
a tremendous beard, asked us where our ship was; and
very charitably hinted that we were deserters, and that if
we did not get along about our business, she would have us
taken up and hanged.

BRISTED, J, *A Pedestrian Tour through part of the Highlands of Scotland in*
1801, London, 1803.

The fact is, some soldiers are to march from this town at
four o'clock this morning, and are unwilling to go to bed
for so few hours; and are therefore dancing in the next
room, while a sans-culotte of a Highlander is regaling
them with his delightful bagpipe... The vile scraping

of the fiddler, might, perhaps, have been endured; but the horrible screaming of the bap-pipe is beyond all tolerance... What a soul, or rather what no soul, must that being have, who delights in such yells, such jarring, such dissonant noises.

BRISTED, J, *A Pedestrian Tour through part of the Highlands of Scotland in 1801*, London, 1803.

The present state of the university, which has now assumed an air and tone, completely in unison with the general dreary, desolate, and decayed condition, of that ancient, large, and once flourishing city.

HALL, J, *Travels in Scotland by an unusual route*, London, 1807.

I was astonished to find, that a barbarous and cruel custom, was so long kept up in this place... the inhabitants here, and all around this part of the country, are in the habit of assembling to see what they term a cat race. The cat is enclosed in an old cask, which is suspended by a rope... and every person on horseback is at liberty... to reach up, and try to knock the end out of the cask... so as to make her fall down among the multitude. He who either kills the cat, or makes her fall among the people, is said to gain the race. Nor is this all: the poor cat... which generally lights on her feet, is chased, taken by the tail, and thrown up into the air, perhaps a hundred times, till she dies... Nor is their goose race, as they call it, less a mark of their humanity. The poor goose is hung by the feet from a gallows... and its neck, being denuded of the feathers, and well soaped or greased to make is slippery, the savages riding below... they try to get hold of its head; and he who pulls off the goose's head, is said to gain the race.

HALL, J, *Travels in Scotland by an unusual route*,
London, 1807.

These mouldering walls have nothing to do with the present... the town is still and lifeless, smitten, as it were, with the curse of eternal silence.

SUTHERLAND, A, *A Summer Ramble in the North Highlands*,
Edinburgh, 1825.

And they have a local pleasure which is as much the staple of the place as old colleges and churches are. This is golfing which is here not a mere pastime, but a business and a passion, and has for ages been so owing probably to their admirable links. This pursuit actually draws many a middle aged gentleman whose stomach requires exercise, and his purse cheap pleasure, to reside here with his family. There is a pretty large set who do nothing else, who begin in the morning and stop only for dinner; and who, after practicing the game, in the sea breeze, all day, discuss it all night. And the result is, that their meetings are very numerous, and that, on the whole, they are rather a guttling population.

COCKBURN, H, *Circuit Journeys by the late Lord Cockburn*,
Edinburgh, 1889.

# St Cyrus, Kincardineshire

The stench of the flax is abominable in these parts, so bad indeed that the odour from fields manured with putrid fish offal, seemed tolerable in comparison.

SOUTHEY, R, *Journal of a tour in Scotland in 1819*, London, 1929.

# St Fillans, Perthshire

The inhabitants are now as fond of their roses and honeysuckles as they formerly were of their dunghills and gutters.

MacCULLOCH, J *The Highlands and Western Isles of Scotland*, London, 1824.

# St Kilda, Outer Hebrides

The inhabitants of the island of St Kilda, to this day, are no better than savages; they are few in number, and live upon stinking fish, and rotten eggs, laid by birds in the hollows of the rocks. They will touch neither eggs nor fish until they are in a state of putrefaction.

MURRAY, S, *A Companion and Useful Guide to the Beauties of Scotland*, London, 1799.

There is one very simple method of catching old birds, known as the gull fishery. An old woman will set long strings with nooses, and then sits watching them, ready to draw them in at the right moment... The oil of the fulmar is coarse and yellow, having a strong rancid smell; the people say it cures rheumatism, and they burn it in their lamps in the long winter nights. The bird is so full of oil, that some slovenly householders do not even extract it, but passing a wick through the body of the dead bird and drawing it out by the beak, actually light the wick thus oiled, and it goes on burning for a considerable time.

GORDON-CUMMING, C, *From the Hebrides to the Himalayas*, London, 1876.

# Stirling, Stirlingshire

Makes an excellent figure at a distance, does not look quite so well as you approach it, and when you come to it, is very wretched indeed.

SKRINE, H, *Tours in the north of England and great part of Scotland*, London, 1795.

The castle is very large, and encloses within its walls a palace... The architecture of this palace is by no means tasteful; the exterior is loaded with several grotesque and ridiculous statues.

DE SAUSSURE, L, *A Voyage to the Hebrides*, London, 1822.

But we were now obliged to leave that pleasant altitude... and descend, through ill-paved stinking streets, to the very earthly necessities of taking our places by an evening coach for Edinburgh.

TOWNSHEND, C, *A Descriptive Tour of Scotland*, London, 1840.

I saw here, for the first time, the beautiful Highland
costume... The Highland garb has this advantage, that
it never embarrasses a lady to have to mention the word
breeches, for the good reason, that the Highlanders have
no breeches... The under garment of the Highlander is very
short, but falls down in many folds, and hence gives the
middle part of the body a certain breadth and fullness. It is
called a kilt. It is made of very heavy material... so that it is
not easily raised by the wind.

KOHL, J, *Travels in Scotland*, London, 1849.

Stirling is a large and, in its present appearance,
uninteresting town.

PEDESTRIAN, *A six weeks' tour in the Highlands of Scotland*,
London, 1851.

The general want of cleanliness, and a total indifference to any
appearance of it, have been very apparent on this day's journey.

SOUTHEY, R, *Journal of a tour in Scotland in* 1819,
London, 1929.

# Stornoway, Outer Hebrides

In the old village of Stornoway, the inside of the house is the
natural and hereditary place of the midden; but were I to tell
you how it is accumulated and managed, I should tell a tale little
fitting for delicate ears, or noses.

MacCULLOCH, J *The Highlands and Western Isles of Scotland*,
London, 1824.

The stranger is surprised at finding so considerable and
flourishing a place in so remote and uninviting a corner...
Stornoway forms a remarkable relief to the prevailing dull,
barren, and dreary appearance of the country.
ANDERSON, G & ANDERSON, P, *Guide to the Highlands and Islands of
Scotland*, London, 1834.

## Stonehaven, Kincardineshire

We put up here to lodge at a doctor's, named Lawson, who
kept a public house, his wife was lame and he none the wisest
of his profession.
VOLUNTEER, *A Journey through part of England and Scotland... in the year
1746*, London, 1747.

There's a small little harbour which they call Steenhive,
but I take the liberty to call it stinking hive, because it's so
unsavoury; which serves only for pirates and pickeroons; but it
bravely accommodates the Highlander for depredations.
FRANCK, R, *Northern Memoirs calculated for the Meridian of Scotland...
writ in the year 1658*, Edinburgh, 1821.

## Strachur, Argyllshire

There was no church, because the minister had gone to the
horse fair at Balloch.
COCKBURN, H, *Circuit Journeys by the late Lord Cockburn*,
Edinburgh, 1889.

# Strathnaver, Sutherland

So from thence we travel into Caithness, and the country of
Strathnaver; where the rude sort of inhabitants dwell, (almost as
barbarous as cannibals) who when they kill a beast, boil him in
his hide, make a cauldron of his skin, broth of his bowels, drink
of his blood, and bread and meat of his carcass.

FRANCK, R, *Northern Memoirs calculated for the Meridian of Scotland...
writ in the year* 1658, Edinburgh, 1821.


# Strathpeffer, Ross and Cromarty

Now the resort of the fair and gay, as well as the
sick and decrepit.

ANDERSON, G & ANDERSON, P, *Guide to the Highlands and Islands of
Scotland*, London, 1834.

Here we are at Strathpeffer, the Harrogate of Scotland,
where people expect their health to be improved by drinking
themselves into a perfect dropsy with nauseous mineral
waters... We had dinner in our own room, so very indifferent,
that it ought to have been hissed off the stage,- a leg of lamb
that might have grown into mutton since the time it was
killed, and a miserable chicken, which had been evidently
starved to death... It was most melancholy and depressing to
observe the crowds of poor, decrepit, miserable objects who
assemble at Strathpeffer.

SINCLAIR, C, *Scotland and the Scotch*, New York, 1840.

# Stronsay, Orkney

On all the ledges of the rocks we observed many nests
of cormorants or shags... our boatmen amused themselves
by dragging down some of the half fledged young with
their boat hooks. These they esteemed very good food;
and we were told, that it is not an uncommon practice to
bury them for four and twenty hours in the earth, which is
said to render them more tender, and to abstract in a great
measure the fishy taste.

NEILL, P, *A Tour through some of the islands of Orkney and Shetland*,
Edinburgh, 1806.

# Sutherland

To traverse Sutherland, hence, in any direction, is to undergo
hunger and fatigue, rain, and wind, and bog, and misery, and
disappointment... The only impression which it has left, is that
of weariness, hunger, and detestation.

MacCULLOCH, J *The Highlands and Western Isles of Scotland*,
London, 1824.

The tourist should make use of his thin veil, with which he
ought to be provided, to protect himself from the attacks
of the myriads of mosquitoes, or midges, which infect the
central and western coasts of Sutherland more than any other
county in Britain. Accustomed as the natives are to their
annoying bites, their patience is often sorely tried by them,

and to strangers the pain inflicted by these little creatures is at first quite excruciating.

ANDERSON, G & ANDERSON, P, *Guide to the Highlands and Islands of Scotland*, London, 1834.

# Tarbet, Dunbartonshire

Not a house you can sleep at.

MURRAY, S, *A Companion and Useful Guide to the Beauties of Scotland*, London, 1799.

The people at the inn stared at us when we spoke, without giving us an answer immediately, which we were at first disposed to attribute to coarseness of manners, but found afterwards that they did not understand us at once, Erse being the language spoken in the family. Nothing but salt meat and eggs for dinner - no potatoes; the house smelt strongly of herrings, which were hung to dry over the kitchen fire.

WORDSWORTH, D, *Recollections of a tour made in Scotland A.D. 1803*. Edinburgh, 1875.

Our boatman lived at the little white house which we saw from the windows... the outside looked comfortable; but within I never saw anything so miserable from dirt, and dirt alone.

WORDSWORTH, D, *Recollections of a tour made in Scotland A.D. 1803*. Edinburgh, 1875.

# Taynuilt, Argyllshire

I admit that the inn at Taynuilt is a vile pot-house; but
the fashion of a breakfast here is not so singular but that
the resemblance may be found in more places that one
in this country.

MacCULLOCH, J *The Highlands and Western Isles of Scotland*,
London, 1824.

The rain drove us back to our inn, which unfortunately is not
of the cleanest, and my prognostics of flea peopled beds (which
you may reckon upon when your inn is a farm house) have
been verified to the letter.

TOWNSHEND, C, *A Descriptive Tour of Scotland*,
London, 1840.

At present that parish has fallen into a state of temporary
heathenism, having only been favoured with miscellaneous
preaching one Sunday in three weeks... so that the
poor, ignorant Highlanders may be apt to say like the
American peasants, 'We are not Christians, because we
have no opportunity.'

SINCLAIR, C, *Scotland and the Scotch*, New York, 1840.

The inn at Taynuilt, was a large but uncomfortable place,
without company, and with the only uncivil domestics we
met during our tour; the maid-servant, an impatient cross
grained being, got completely out of temper because we
laughed when she brought in a mountain of oat cakes for tea,

and grumbled sadly, when we sent her to seek
some wheat bread.

PEDESTRIAN, *A six weeks' tour in the Highlands of Scotland*,
London, 1851.

# Thurso, Caithness

Thurso is about the same size as Wick, and equally dirty
and irregularly built.

SUTHERLAND, A, *A Summer Ramble in the North Highlands*,
Edinburgh, 1825.

# Tillicoultry, Clackmannanshire

Tillicoultry, a parish in this neighbourhood, I found, had
been rather unfortunate in its clergymen. One of these having
lived much respected among his parishioners for fifteen
years, lost his living for having been too familiar with his
maid servant. The parishioners... advised his successor to
marry... but he would not... he was also obliged to give up his
living; his maid servant either having been seduced by him,
or been the seducer.

HALL, J, *Travels in Scotland by an unusual route*,
London, 1807.

# Tobermory, Mull, Argyllshire

We got on board our vessel... Our crew consisted of the captain, a man, and a boy. The first was a short, thick, dark man, whose eye (as we found to our cost) belied him not when it indicated fraud and cunning. The boy, his son, was an ill-favoured animal, with a complexion of a toady yellow, and a skin which, though not marked with the small pox, was fretted all over, like a certain cheese, of a hot and gaping quality.

TOWNSHEND, C, *A Descriptive Tour of Scotland*, London, 1840.

# Tomintoul, Banffshire

Tomintoul is a dull, miserable place, apparently falling rapidly into decay.

SUTHERLAND, A, *A Summer Ramble in the North Highlands*, Edinburgh, 1825.

# Tranent, East Lothian

An old decayed town... I had heard much of their cookery, and did not care how little they showed their skill in it.

LONDONER, *North of England and Scotland in* 1704, Edinburgh, 1818.

# Tummel Bridge, Perthshire

When we arrived at our solitary inn, fully expecting
a comfortable gratification to our craving appetites,
we were mortified in the want of proper necessaries;
nothing to eat, with bad tea, but some coarse, indigestible
barley cakes; oaten bread would now have been
a comparative luxury.

SHAW, S, *A Tour, in 1787, from London to the Western Highlands of
Scotland*, London, 1788.

We... entered a large house, where we were presented with
a perfect Highland scene... Three women with very dirty
visages peeping from out their long, matted, dishevelled,
and uncombed locks of yellow... were walking leisurely to
and fro, in a large apartment, hung round with diverse and
sundry articles of food, as dried meat, onions, sugar &c. &c.
suspended on nails in a row... This room was also furnished
with old, shabby, dirty, broken chairs, stools, and tables,
under which last lay... no less than nine dogs of different
genera, which soon filled us entirely with fleas and other
vermin, to our sore annoyance and discomfiture... I... began
to write in my diary, during which I had the satisfaction of
observing that the youthful and blooming hostess, without
any ceremony, undressed herself close by me... and deposited
herself in the bed at my side... At length was brought us by the
old hag... some stale bannock which we could not swallow...
a dab of butter on a broken saucer, whose colour the dirt
concealed; after which she laid down on the table, without
a plate or dish, some slices of hung beef, which required an

ocean of liquid to wash away the saline and pungent effects of one mouthful... We were then shown... into a large upper room... at whose window bench were standing, more than half drunk, three stout strapping Highlanders, with very short kilts, not reaching down so low as cleverly and fairly to cover their posteriors... At breakfast, as we could not eat the bannock, which seemed to be composed of barley meal, barley straw, and dirt... we were favoured with a very small portion of the stalest bread I ever saw.

BRISTED, J, *A Pedestrian Tour through part of the Highlands of Scotland in 1801*, London, 1803.

# Turriff, Aberdeenshire

A cheerful village... Like the majority of small towns in Scotland, however, it does not sustain this favourable impression on closer inspection.

SUTHERLAND, A, *A Summer Ramble in the North Highlands*, Edinburgh, 1825.

# Tyndrum, Perthshire

Tyndrum, the ramifying point on the road to Glencoe, is noted, only for the dreary aspect of its position, and, if it is not changed since my day, for its unspeakable badness and dirt as an inn.

MacCULLOCH, J *The Highlands and Western Isles of Scotland*, London, 1824.

In no country through which I have travelled, have I met with so many highway robbers, (in an equal space), as between Tyndrum and Dunkeld. We had scarcely left the former place, when we were stopped, in broad daylight, and robbed on the king's highway. This happened several times afterwards, in the course of two days.

JOHNSON, J, *The Recess or Autumnal relaxations in the Highlands and Lowlands*, London, 1834.

The dwellings of the people in Tyndrum proper, that is, the holes in which they burrow, are disgraceful, and nearly inconceivable, even in Scotland.

COCKBURN, H, *Circuit Journeys by the late Lord Cockburn*, Edinburgh, 1889.

The house at Tyndrum stands alone; at a little distance there is a wretched assemblage of hovels called Clifton.

SOUTHEY, R, *Journal of a tour in Scotland in 1819*, London, 1929.

# Ulva, Isle of Mull, Argyllshire

Every laird in the Hebrides has his piper... We were regaled with this music at Ulva House every day during dinner, and although the piper was placed outside of the house, it was almost impossible to hear the conversation.

DE SAUSSURE, L, *A Voyage to the Hebrides*, London, 1822.

# Weem, Aberfeldy, Perthshire

The small inn at Weem, when I was at it, was not
a good house.

MURRAY, S, *A Companion and Useful Guide to the Beauties of Scotland,*
London, 1799.

# Western Isles, Outer Hebrides

The people in England, and indeed the southern parts of
Scotland, have scarcely any conception how hardy those
who live in the northern and mountainous parts are. In the
Western Isles, women are sometimes seen suckling their
children while wading up to their knees in snow, without either
shoes or stockings.

HALL, J, *Travels in Scotland by an unusual route,*
London, 1807.

# West Tarbert, Kintyre, Argyllshire

The village seemed to have poured its entire population to
gaze at the steamer's company; several in the crowd were
good looking and well dressed females... they seemed to the
eye of a stranger as out of place, as an Englishman would be
among a crowd of Arabs, or an European consorting with the
Chinese or Laplanders... many of us wondered how civilized
beings, educated, perhaps brought up in the Lowlands, could
live among such a rude rough population; or find companions

fitted to their pleasing appearance among the uncivilized looking people, who surrounded them.

PEDESTRIAN, *A six weeks' tour in the Highlands of Scotland*, London, 1851.

# Wick, Caithness

The streets, like those in most other ancient burghs, require more frequent visits from the scavenger's brush.

SUTHERLAND, A, *A Summer Ramble in the North Highlands*, Edinburgh, 1825.

Wick lies low, and in a dirty situation; and, but for the stream which passes through it, and the sharp breezes of the north, the smell of its fish and garbage would be intolerable.

ANDERSON, G & ANDERSON, P, *Guide to the Highlands and Islands of Scotland*, London, 1834.

Wick, at any time, cannot be a lovely town; but during the herring fishing it is odious. The stationary population of 6,722 souls is increased during the fishing season to upwards of 16,000, and as the houses do not increase in the same proportion, and the sanitary arrangements are not of the highest order of excellence, you may imagine that this great influx of population is not calculated to improve the appearance of Wick. As may be supposed, considerable drunkenness and immorality prevails at Wick during the fishing season... Wick harbour is surrounded on the land side by hundreds of erections... these are the gutting troughs. Round them stood rows of what close inspection led you to conclude were women, though at first sight you might be excused for having some doubts respecting their sex... For although the majority of the 2,500 women employed in gutting herrings are certainly not lovely nor delicate limbed, still I observed several pretty and modest looking girls who would apparently have made better shepherdesses than fish gutters.

WELD, C, *Two months in the Highlands, Orcadia, and Skye*, London, 1860.

Scotch kirks, as the English tourist to Caledonia knows to his sorrow, are sorry affairs, and that at Wick forms no exception to the rule. There is nothing to be seen in Wick church.

WELD, C, *Two months in the Highlands, Orcadia, and Skye*, London, 1860.

# Yell, Shetland

Yell is a dull, uninteresting island.

ANDERSON, G & ANDERSON, P, *Guide to the Highlands and Islands of Scotland*, London, 1834.

# **Luath** Press Limited

*committed to publishing well written books worth reading*

LUATH PRESS takes its name from Robert Burns, whose little collie Luath (*Gael.*, swift or nimble) tripped up Jean Armour at a wedding and gave him the chance to speak to the woman who was to be his wife and the abiding love of his life. Burns called one of the 'Twa Dogs' Luath after Cuchullin's hunting dog in Ossian's *Fingal*.

Luath Press was established in 1981 in the heart of Burns country, and is now based a few steps up the road from Burns' first lodgings on Edinburgh's Royal Mile. Luath offers you distinctive writing with a hint of unexpected pleasures.

Most bookshops in the UK, the US, Canada, Australia, New Zealand and parts of Europe, either carry our books in stock or can order them for you. To order direct from us, please send a £sterling cheque, postal order, international money order or your credit card details (number, address of cardholder and expiry date) to us at the address below. Please add post and packing as follows: UK – £1.00 per delivery address; overseas surface mail – £2.50 per delivery address; overseas airmail – £3.50 for the first book to each delivery address, plus £1.00 for each additional book by airmail to the same address. If your order is a gift, we will happily enclose your card or message at no extra charge.

**Luath** Press Limited
543/2 Castlehill
The Royal Mile
Edinburgh EH1 2ND
Scotland
Telephone: +44 (0)131 225 4326 (24 hours)
email: sales@luath.co.uk
Website: www.luath.co.uk